MONTGOMERY COLLEGE LIBRARY
ROCKVILLE CAMPUS

AN INTRODUCTION TO
SHAKESPEARE'S COMEDIES

By the same author

GEORGE ELIOT: MIDDLEMARCH: A CASEBOOK *(editor)*
UNOFFICIAL SELVES: CHARACTER IN THE NOVEL
FROM DICKENS TO THE PRESENT DAY

AN INTRODUCTION TO SHAKESPEARE'S COMEDIES

PATRICK SWINDEN

BARNES & NOBLE
BOOKS·
10 East 53d St., New York 10022
(a division of Harper & Row Publishers, Inc.)

© Patrick Swinden 1973

All rights reserved. No part of this publication may
be reproduced or transmitted, in any form or by
any means, without permission.

First published in the United Kingdom 1973 by
The Macmillan Press Ltd

Published in the U.S.A. 1973 by
HARPER & ROW PUBLISHERS, INC.
BARNES & NOBLE IMPORT DIVISION

ISBN 06-496673-9 mc 78 - 1733

Printed in Great Britain

Preface

I make two claims for this book. It is short, and it is what its title proclaims it to be.

Brevity is the soul of wit, and to write about Shakespeare's comedies without wit would go a long way towards defeating the object of the exercise. I hope this book increases the reader's enjoyment as well as his understanding of Shakespeare. Since the chapters are short he will be able to take time off to test the judgements they contain against another reading of the appropriate play, or part of a play.

Because this book is an introduction to the comedies, it does not assume that its readers will have read widely within the vast range of Shakespeare scholarship and criticism. It is assumed only that the principal plays have been read or seen on the stage. When a critic's name is mentioned, I try to explain the view he takes of the play under discussion, in so far as this promotes understanding of the argument that is being advanced.

One more word before the acknowledgements. I have not seen fit to enter into a discussion about the nature of comedy. My business is with the plays, not with ideas of a general nature which can be apprehended through them, and I have rarely found a critic who has not bogged down his argument about a particular play when he has ventured into the quicksands of this sort of definition. In my opening chapter I do have something to say about what is distinctive about Shakespeare's comedies. On the wider issue of what is distinctive about comedy itself, I would make just three tentative observations. A work of art that is comic usually ends happily. Except where it is satirical, the aesthetic delight it provokes in its audience is usually unmixed with critical reservations. Some of the time, it makes us laugh; and even if it doesn't make us laugh, it makes us happy.

I should be prepared to say that to the extent that these properties apply to a play, it is comic; to the extent that they do not apply it is not comic. I am not prepared to be more precise than that.

There are two books which I think are very helpful in complementing what I have to say about the comedies. The first is F. E. Halliday, *A Shakespeare Companion*, from which I have not felt ashamed to borrow useful information about the plays. The second is C. L. Barber, *Shakespeare's Festive Comedy*, the most valuable commentary I have read on the early and middle comedies. I owe to Professor Barber much of my understanding of 'where to start', and recommend to my readers that they consult his book for evidence, where they feel that my comments on staging, festivity, audience response are insufficient. Other debts are listed in the text or in the short bibliography at the end of the book.

I should like to mention two more personal debts, to D. J. Palmer and J. Norton Smith. I have also to thank my wife who, as always, has contributed much to my understanding of the subject and to whatever grace there is in my expression of it. Mrs Nancy Walsh and Mrs Shelagh Aston corrected and typed the manuscript with their customary speed and efficiency.

August 1973   P.S.

Contents

APPROXIMATE ORDER OF COMPOSITION OF SHAKESPEARE'S WORKS

PERIOD	COMEDIES	HISTORIES	TRAGEDIES
1584 I	The Comedy of Errors The Taming of the Shrew The Two Gentlemen of Verona	1, 2, 3 Henry VI Richard III King John	Titus Andronicus
1592			
	Love's Labour's Lost	Venus and Adonis ⎱ poems Rape of Lucrece ⎰	
1594	A Midsummer Night's Dream	Richard II	Romeo and Juliet
II	The Merchant of Venice The Merry Wives of Windsor Much Ado About Nothing As You Like it	1 Henry IV 2 Henry IV Henry V	
1599	Twelfth Night Troilus and Cressida Measure for Measure All's Well That Ends Well		Julius Caesar Hamlet Othello Timon of Athens King Lear Macbeth Antony and Cleopatra Coriolanus
III			
1608			
IV	Pericles Cymbeline The Winter's Tale The Tempest	Henry VIII	
1613			

A Note on Dates and Texts

The edition of Shakespeare's plays which comes most readily to hand is that of Peter Alexander, published by Collins in 1951. Since it is also a very good edition I have used it throughout, in spite of the occasional preference I have entertained for the reading of a part of one or other of the plays in a separate edition under the New Cambridge, Arden, Signet and Penguin imprints. This makes for a simplification I feel is desirable in a book of this kind.

Another matter I have simplified is the dates of the plays. Often it is not possible for scholars to provide a definite date for a Shakespeare play, and in any case complications must arise from the time lapse between the writing, production, and printing of separate (and sometimes very different) versions of a play. On occasion Shakespeare appears to have adapted a play to suit a different occasion from that of its first production (see my comment on *A Midsummer Night's Dream*), in which case one has to bear in mind two separate dates for a single play. If Shakespeare wrote other plays between the date of original composition and the date of revision, then each of them might be deemed either earlier or later, depending on the scholar's or editor's or critic's view of the importance of the revision. Clearly we cannot worry overmuch about these matters in an introduction to the comedies. I have felt justified in taking over Alexander's chronology, which I reproduce opposite. It has the advantage of specifying only approximate dates and, by providing separate columns for comedies, histories and tragedies, an approximate sequence also. I should mention the three assumptions which acceptance of Alexander's dates has allowed me to make, and which not every critic would agree with: first, that *The Taming of the Shrew* follows immediately after *The Comedy of Errors*;

second, that *A Midsummer Night's Dream* was written later than *Romeo and Juliet*; and third, that *All's Well that Ends Well* was written later than *Measure for Measure*. None of these assumptions, I think, affects the substance of my argument about the plays concerned.

I

The Spirit of Shakespearean Comedy

In tragedy he often writes with a great appearance of toil and study, what is written at last with little felicity; but in his comick scenes, he seems to produce without labour, what no labour can improve. In tragedy he is always struggling after some occasion to be comick, but in comedy he seems to repose, or to luxuriate, as in a mode of thinking congenial to his nature. In his tragick scenes there is always something wanting, but his comedy often surpasses expectation or desire. His comedy pleases by the thoughts and the language, and his tragedy for the greater part by incident and action. His tragedy seems to be skill, his comedy to be instinct.

That was what Dr Johnson wrote about Shakespeare when he was preparing his edition of the plays in 1765. It is not what we should expect to hear from a modern editor or, for that matter, from many people who enjoy Shakespeare, who read him and go to see the plays in the theatre today. In fact I have the impression that Shakespeare's comedies – the 'straight' comedies, not the so-called problem plays like *Measure for Measure*, or the final plays like *The Winter's Tale* – are an embarrassment to his admirers. What are they to make of the improbable co-incidences and the impossible disguisings, the imperceptive heroes and the boys dressed up as girls and the girls dressed up as boys whom they fail to perceive? It is all so silly. Even so, Johnson admired them. He thought Shakespeare had an instinctive preference for comedy. And Johnson was a man who was not easily pleased. Six years before his edition of Shakespeare was published he had written *Rasselas*, a grave and, some would say, pessimistic inquiry into the nature of human ambition – not at all silly and, unfortunately, not at all improbable either. If the comedies were not an embarrassment to the author of *Rasselas*, there is no reason why they should be to us.

Johnson's view is supported by the number of comedies Shakespeare wrote. If we discount *Henry IV* Parts 1 and 2 as hybrids of comedy and history, then Shakespeare wrote as many comedies as he wrote histories and tragedies put together. In other words, Shakespeare seems to have enjoyed writing comedy, since we have no evidence to lead us to suppose that his audience preferred comedy to either of the other forms, and therefore demanded more of it at their expense. One of the things everybody knows about Shakespeare is that like his contemporary, Christopher Marlowe, he incorporated a fair amount of comedy into his tragedies proper – the gravediggers in *Hamlet*, the fool in *King Lear*. What they often do *not* realise is how comic are some of the tragic heroes themselves. Hamlet, Lear and Cleopatra are just three obvious examples of tragic protagonists who encourage us to respond to what they do on a knife edge of laughter and horror. Anyone who fails to muster an embarrassed giggle (at least) whilst watching some of Hamlet's exchanges with Polonius, or Lear's with Gloucester on the hillside near Dover, is not responding to the full range of meanings either of those plays is offering. In many of the comedies, as we shall see, this kind of thing works in reverse. The comic action often teeters perilously on the brink of disaster. Perhaps this is the wrong image, suggesting as it does the antics of a silent screen comedian like Harold Lloyd dangling from a clock hand or tip-toeing along a girder. Comic suspense of any kind is rare in Shakespeare, or at any rate of subsidiary importance. Instead there is something in the mood of the comedy which threatens to infect it, which throws mysterious shadows over what would otherwise be the intolerable uniformity of its brightness.

The sadness and pathos and other kinds of disturbance that have a place in so many of the comedies, I shall discuss at the appropriate time. For the present it will be as well to be warned that we can place too much emphasis upon them. A modern audience tends to light up at moments like that in *Much Ado about Nothing* where Beatrice orders Benedick to 'Kill Claudio' or in *The Merchant of Venice* where Shylock expresses the view that, though a Jew, he is as much a man as any of the worldly Venetians who taunt and despise him. The one converts a courtly game into a serious conflict of loyalties; the other alerts the audience to tragic propensities in a comic villain. No doubt this was always the case. Neither of these events does anything for a modern audience that it would not have done for Shakespeare's own. But modern audiences are notoriously unsusceptible to the courtly games out of which events like these arise. *The Two Gentlemen of Verona* is, admittedly, one of the feeblest, if not the feeblest, of the comedies. Even so, one might have supposed that the comic business thrust into it in a production by the Royal Shakespeare Company a couple of years ago – high jinks and hippies prancing around a swimming pool – was not absolutely necessary to engage the audience's attention. So often prestige productions in recent years have taken the form of a visual and/or linguistic restructuring of the bulk of whatever comedy it happens to be, around the unchanged, 'dramatic' pivot upon which the whole action is presumed to turn. Somehow or other you have to 'get through' all those mistaken identities and maskings and unmaskings so that the correct *frisson* will be achieved in the central scenes. The Elizabethans would not have felt the need to be apologetic about these things. Beatrice's big scene, as well as Shylock's, would have taken its place, important as it might have been in the unfolding of the play's design, along with much else that we tend to depress, distort, or simply 'cut' – because it doesn't satisfy our demands as to what the drama is about.

We call each example of the dramatist's art a 'play'. It is a fact of theatrical history that the common sense of that word has become less and less appropriate to what happens on the stage from the Elizabethan period to almost the present day. There is very little impression, for example, of play in the domestic dramas of the Victorian playwrights in this country, or of Henrik Ibsen further afield. The idea of playing games on the stage is still foreign to most people, including many of those who espouse it most fervently. But it is gaining ground and, ironically, it has been applied to the staging of Shakespeare's plays. Ironically because the games have consisted so frequently of fooling about with the audience's expectations of what should be happening, and thereby transforming the play into little more than raw material out of which the producer can construct something new. Usually Shakespeare's lines still manage to get in the way and turn the whole thing into a fiasco. It is a pity this has to happen, because Shakespeare's plays do themselves so often have a pronounced element of the 'game' in them, and it is a game to which a modern audience can still respond. In my experience, producers and actors of the comedies rarely manage to bring the games to life. They either complicate things by imposing their own rules; or they play it straight – i.e. as a period piece. In the first instance the rules are strictly inapplicable to this particular game; in the second, the period didn't play plays straight anyway. This is why modern productions of the comedies are usually incomprehensible, dull, or both.

There are plenty of games in the comedies – plays within plays, masques, even a wrestling match in *As You Like It.* Let us take a look at one of them, at the opening of the second act of *Much Ado about Nothing.* Claudio is in love with Hero, and has appointed Don Pedro to woo her for him. Benedick and Beatrice are still at loggerheads, neither having disclosed his or her love for the other, or indeed recognised that he (or she) is in love. The young men enter as masked revellers, and the question we ask is, how seriously are we to take the disguises they have contrived? Is there any art to see the mind's construction in the face when it is 'covered' by a mask? Hero mistakes Don Pedro for Claudio. Two minor characters, Balthasar and Margaret, seem to know each other; though two others, Antonio and Ursula, do not. Benedick and Beatrice know each other but pretend not to. A little later, Don John, the villain, recognises Claudio easily enough (his friend Borachio knows him by his bearing) but for his own purposes addresses him as Benedick. Claudio accepts his mistake and falls in with it. Even when we make allowances for Don Pedro's imitation of Claudio – in his clothes as well as his bearing, no doubt – we are bound to agree that Shakespeare wants it both ways. For the part of the plot involving Claudio, Don Pedro and Hero, it is important the characters should not be able to pierce the disguise. On the other hand, for the part of the plot involving Benedick and Beatrice, it is important they should. The behaviour of the minor characters reinforces this theatrical duplicity. The two actions are quite inconsistent. Shakespeare shouldn't be able to have both of them in the same play, let alone in the same scene.

The obvious answer is that masking is a convention of the

Elizabethan theatre and we have to suppose that characters really could mistake one another's identities when they were masked; just as, in the tragedies, characters could be made to eavesdrop on one half of a scene and not the other (Othello on Cassio and Bianca) or mistake one man's writing for another's (Gloucester mistakes Edmund's for Edgar's in *King Lear*). With this explanation we could no doubt go on to discriminate between the characters of the main participants in respect of the use they make of the convention. Naturally Hero doesn't see through Don Pedro's disguise, because she isn't very intelligent. Beatrice and Benedick are both intelligent, and that explains why they *do* see through each other. At a pinch, one might say the same for Balthasar and Margaret. But this is to turn the game to earnest prematurely. What Shakespeare does is to put a single game to at least two uses. The playfulness of it all provides excuse enough. So, for the purposes of the plot, Hero must mistake Don Pedro for Claudio. For rather different purposes, and rather more sophisticated ones, Benedick and Beatrice must see through each other's disguises; because when they have done so, they each – Benedick especially – run into another disguise, the verbal one that stimulates at the same time as it perplexes feeling. Benedick lays himself wide open when he asks Beatrice, under pretence of being someone else, what Benedick is. 'Why he is the Prince's jester, a very dull fool' etc. It is only a slightly more complicated game than the one they play unmasked. So, what the audience is encouraged to do is to switch over from one set of expectations to another in mid-scene. The information that is to be transmitted determines the use to which the masking game is put. In the first instance that information is mechanical: we have to see Hero mistaking Don Pedro for Claudio and, for the moment, we have to be uncertain as to whether the Duke is really wooing on Claudio's behalf, or on his own. It is all a matter of quite superficial plotting, with little interest in the characters behind the masks. In the second instance the information has more to do with the dispositions of the characters. We have to see them disclosing their feelings under the protection afforded by the game. They are sparring with each other as before, but the pretence of a different identity allows more to slip out – to us and to the other party, though it is 'taken' differently by each – than was possible earlier in the play.

The scene opens with a drum beating, is conducted in a highly formal manner – the speeches are punctuated with lines that obviously close one 'sub-scene' and open another: ' "Speak low, if you speak love" *Takes her aside*.' – and ends with a dance. It is clearly artificial and stylised, and we are expected to enjoy it as such. We notice the way the narrative is developed, and we muse on the possibilities opening up in the relationship between Benedick and Beatrice. But to emphasise these narrative and 'character' functions at the expense of our participation in a game is to misunderstand what is going on and our relation to it. The same is true of the much more important game near the heart of the play – the trick that is played on Benedick and Beatrice by Don Pedro and the rest. This occupies two long scenes; and the equally game-like consequence, as the lovers are driven to express their love for each other, occupies a third. In fact *Much Ado* relies more heavily on narrative and intrigue than its sister comedies do. *As You Like It*, and even *Twelfth Night*, are not so dependent. But even in *Much Ado* we ignore the element of game and play at some cost to our sense of satisfaction with the play as a whole.

$$\star \quad \star \quad \star \quad \star \quad \star$$

This is even more important when we speculate upon the circumstances in which the comedies were originally produced. No one knows enough about this, but a good deal of evidence has been advanced to support the view that many of the comedies were written to grace a particular occasion, a festive occasion either seasonal or personal. Leslie Hotson wrote a whole book (*First Night of Twelfth Night*) to try to prove this was true of just one of the plays, and I am bound to say his argument had a mixed, often hostile, reception. But I should like to think, even if Mr Hotson is mistaken in the assumption he makes about the specific occasion Shakespeare was writing for, that there was an occasion of some sort, and that *Twelfth Night* was by no means unusual in this respect. I should be very surprised if *Love's Labour's Lost*, *A Midsummer Night's Dream*, *Twelfth Night* and *The Tempest* were not first produced at the request of some company or household which had an occasion of one kind or another to celebrate. And there is a story that Queen Elizabeth herself ordered Shakespeare to write *The Merry Wives of*

Windsor so that Falstaff would not disappear from the stage for ever after his despondent exit in Act v of *Henry IV Part 2*.

Of course, even if this were certainly the case, Shakespeare was a businessman as well as a poet and dramatist. He would want to be sure that what he wrote would be a saleable commodity on the public as well as the private stage. Plays that had been privately commissioned would have been written with an eye to the way they could be produced later at whichever theatre his company was using at the time, with or without additions and adaptations. There are hints of such adaptations in some of the versions of the plays we have, though the adaptations may have been the other way round – to make plays previously enacted before the public suitable for private performance. This certainly happened when *The Tempest* was performed at Whitehall in May 1613, to celebrate the marriage of Princess Elizabeth and the Elector Palatine. The most interesting example of such adaptation is *A Midsummer Night's Dream*, which was acted before a court audience in 1604 and which may have been performed for the first time at the wedding of the Earl of Derby and Elizabeth Vere in 1595. Professor John Dover Wilson, the editor of the New Cambridge edition of the play, argued that Shakespeare made several important additions to the fifth act and that these additions had to do with the different requirements of 'occasional' and public performance. It is this sort of thing, combined with what I think is very strong internal evidence, which makes the supposition that at least some of the plays were written for special occasions a sensible one.

In writing this book I have assumed that even if Shakespeare did not write many of his comedies for immediate private performance, he did have his eye on a private audience of some kind – to be satisfied at a later date, perhaps, after a few cuts and additions in the right places. Probably some of them were written in the first place to celebrate an occasion, in which case the matter would have to be appropriate, sometimes quite explicitly so. This has not been proved in any single instance. The first play that we know was written for a noble wedding, for example, is Samuel Daniel's *Hymen's Triumph* – in 1614, at least eighteen years after the *Dream* was first produced. Nevertheless it is at least as sound an assumption as that the reverse is true: that all Shakespeare's comedies were written deliberately and exclusively for the public stage and that Shakespeare was not at all concerned with the possibilities (above all financial) of private performance. This is the assumption that underlies most people's views on the comedies. I think it is why they are usually produced so unimaginatively.

It makes a big difference. Think of going to see a play at the theatre today. You take your seat, probably at the other side of a proscenium arch with a battery of lights separating you from the players. You probably know none of the members of the audience around you, and if you do you are cut off from them by the prevailing darkness. You can respond with the audience as a whole, and the actors on the stage can respond to you as a member of that audience as a whole. But by and large it is an experience which is anonymous, one which you have as a member of a group within which few members are known to one another. In the Elizabethan public playhouse – the Theatre, the Curtain, the Globe – this would not be so pronounced. This is not the place to describe all the features of the Elizabethan playhouse, but the combination of apron stage, visible separation of members of the audience according to their social position, and daylight performances, must have helped to make the audience more conscious of itself, of the separate identities of its constituents, and the players and the audience more aware of each other. In the smaller area of the private theatre, these relationships would be even more pronounced, most members of the audience would know one another, and the playwright and players would know beforehand of at least some members of the audience. The effect this had on the way the play was played must have been considerable.

In some respects these effects are not to our present advantage. *Love's Labour's Lost* was almost certainly written for an audience of *cognoscenti* fascinated by contemporary fashions in dress, language and sentiment. Unfortunately, the shape of a new doublet, a new Euphuism or a new sonnet is no longer a living issue, and we have to delve far below the surface of the play before we arrive at anything of lasting value. *Troilus and Cressida* may have been acted privately at the Middle Temple, in which case the distinctively 'learned' style in which it is written might be attributed to Shakespeare's exertions to satisfy the clever young men at the Inns of Court who would have comprised its audience. Modern ears are less impressed by the 'corresponsive and fulfilling bolts', 'the princes orgillous', 'grain tortive' and other equally indigestible latinisms and legalisms the play is crammed with. They represent the debit side of private performance, and they are what strike us immediately when reading the play.

There is usually a credit side as well. The trouble is that reading often fails to bring it out. It should come out in performance, where the gestures and movements which the words are there to prompt can be made to emerge from the rubble and point up the play's direction. *Troilus and Cressida* is a special case, and I don't think much is to be gained by dealing with it along with the other 'comedies'. But *Love's Labour's Lost* gains enormously from staging. Nothing can save much of the literary satire, which is hopelessly dated. What can be saved is the celebratory nature of the play, within which the satire is only one of a number of incidental counter-attractions. By this I mean that a good production should be capable of putting us in a position in which we can enjoy the games that the play dissolves into in Act v almost in the same way as the characters do. By the time we have entered Act v we have become so involved in the intrigues between the King of Navarre and the Princess of France, and their various attendants and servants, that we feel able to participate with them in the masque of the Muscovites, the pageant of the Nine Worthies, and the Spring and Winter songs. The way in which, earlier in the play, characters have moved away from the centre of the action to a position not so very different from our own, as a second audience breaking down the clear division between stage and auditorium, encourages us to assume a kind of complicity with the stage characters, and with that complicity, enjoyment.

The ability of the actors to achieve a *rapport* with members of the audience is crucial in producing a state of affairs where this is possible. One theory about the circumstances in which *Love's Labour's Lost* was produced is that it was written during the year 1593–4 when the plague was raging in London and the theatrical companies left the capital to tour the provinces. There they entertained members of the nobility and their following in the enormous gabled houses that were rising over much of the country throughout the Tudor period. It is suggested that the play we have is a revision of an earlier version that was acted at this time in the Earl of Southampton's house. The Earl you may remember as the favoured candidate for W. H., the dedicatee of Shakespeare's sonnets (which were being written at about the same time), and thus, quite possibly, the poet's patron and friend throughout most of the 1590s. Certainly the nobility would have required plays to entertain them during this dark period. And who more satisfactorily than Shakespeare, who had already written at least three very popular plays – *Henry VI Part 1*, *Titus Andronicus* and *The Taming of the Shrew* – by this time? If *Love's Labour's Lost* were written to serve such an occasion it would explain the ease and freedom with which it handles the love affairs of young noblemen, and the sense of involvement we feel as privileged beings in the action that is unfolding on-stage. It would also explain its difference in this respect from the three earlier comedies, about which I shall have something to say in Chapter 2.

Private performance, then, tends to provoke two important changes in the way the play makes its effect. It encourages the playwright to indulge in coterie jokes and references, and this works against our enjoyment of the play so many hundreds of years after the business the jokes and references depend on has ceased to be of any interest. On the other hand it allows the playwright and his company to establish a *rapport* with an audience composed of persons whose identities they know, which is very much more immediate and discriminating than in the public playhouse. In dealing with the plays separately I shall have something to say about how this *rapport* works in detail, about the way the audience or sections of it or individual members of it are given privileged positions, special roles at one point or another in the action. In the meantime let me finish what I have to say about this matter by reminding you that if an individual, or several individuals, are singled out from a larger group for special attention, then the members of the larger group themselves take up a different position from the one they occupied before. In twentieth-century music hall, where a member of the audience is addressed individually from the stage, the rest of the audience are simultaneously shut off from participating directly in what is going on and alerted to the fact that they are in a vulnerable position. Any one of them might be at the receiving end next time. The same with the request for volunteers in a conjuring trick or an exhibition of mesmerism. A time arrives when the distinction between stage and auditorium breaks down and, equally important, the audience is made aware of itself as composed of both individuals and fluid groupings. Nothing could be further away from the nineteenth-century stage or present-day television drama. Nothing could be further away, either, from much contemporary thrust stage productions which insist upon anonymous 'participation' from the audience. Everybody now knows that the first of these comments is true, but the truth of the second is slow to sink in. How to convince a public, fee-paying audience that each of its members enjoys an in-dividual, group and mass experience, was a problem Shakespeare managed to overcome in transferring comedy from the private to the public stage. Modern producers, on the whole, still have to learn how. They particularly have to learn how in their productions of Shakespearean comedy.

It is more important in comedy than tragedy. In tragedy the audience's attention is much more firmly riveted to the per-sonality of the central figure, the tragic protagonist. He is played off against a background of subsidiary characters any one of whom is less charismatic than himself. Margaret stands up to Richard in the first act of *Richard III*, but she dwindles into the role of 'wailing queen dominant' after I, iii. No one at the court of Elsinore can vie with Hamlet for the centre of the stage, and no one on the heath can stand up to Lear's terrific outbursts. In some of the tragedies one other character achieves a kind of prominence by acting as a stimulant to activity in the hero. He provides a gravitational field within which the tensions generated in the hero can be visibly demonstrated. Iago is the most obvious example of this kind of character. Edmund in *King Lear* is a run-down version of it. Lady Macbeth takes on the role in the first acts of *Macbeth* and then gradually fades away until her sleep-walking scene in Act V. These characters are principally mechanisms which enable the hero to show himself to his best advantage. Since the Romantics they have appeared to be a great deal more than that, usurping too much of the centre of the stage. In fact, though they are active and busy – i.e. they are given plenty of stage business – they should not seriously deflect attention from the hero. Our eye is not encouraged to dart about amongst the *dramatis personae* as it is in the comedies. Or where it does, as in *Troilus and Cressida*, it detracts from the power of the play as a whole.

The comedies do not have central characters like this. Although some characters, like Berowne, and Rosalind, have a great deal to say for themselves, they do not subordinate others to dependent positions as the tragic protagonists do. For a start, their actions do not usually precipitate the plot. As far as the plot is concerned, Berowne is just one of the four academicians who falls in love with one of the four girls. Rosalind enters the forest of Arden, but what she discovers there is not of her own making. Othello, Lear and Antony visibly create the circumstances in which they and the rest of the cast find themselves. The people who create the plots of the comedies are distinctly inferior creatures: Egeus, Don John, Oliver and Duke Frederick for example – characters whose very names we easily forget, and whose presence on the stage is usually brief. Also, the links between the groups of characters are generally weakened in the comedies. The minor characters in the tragedies are always locked firmly into place. At some point they affect the fortunes of the hero in a very direct way. Characters belonging to a distinct group on-stage at some time or other detach themselves from it and acquire an effective part in the hero's own action. Lady Macbeth, Banquo, Macduff all exert pressures on the main plot of *Macbeth* at different times and in different ways.

The same thing does not happen in the comedies. Their structure is very different. Typically, it takes the form of a medley of separate actions, all of which have some bearing on the main preoccupations of the play. Because these separate actions take place in the same locality or localities, actors in them will cross one another's paths from time to time, and complications may ensue. Usually, however, these are only momentary complications. They are unknotted long before the end of the play. There are two exceptions to this. One is *A Midsummer Night's Dream*, and there are special reasons for it that I shall discuss in my chapter on the play. The other is *Twelfth Night* (Viola's involvement with Sir Andrew Aguecheek, culminating in the duel) but that is more apparent than real, a much slighter thing than it may appear looking back on the play from a distance.

So in the comedies our attention is dispersed amongst a number of characters occupying positions in clearly demarcated groups and narrative sequences. The firm ground on which we stand in relation to what is happening on the stage, which we exercise in watching a tragedy, is denied us. Our responses therefore do not have to be more profound, but they do have to be more mobile. When Hamlet meets the gravedigger, the gravedigger is almost immediately absorbed into the train of the hero's thoughts and sensations; and since we are so attentive to the hero, we too are able to absorb him into the prevailing tone of the play. But when Bottom finds himself with Titania and the fairies, and the mechanicals find themselves cheek by jowl with the courtiers, there is no blending of the different parts of the play into a homogeneous whole. The separate parts are obstinately recalcitrant, and the mood of the play, its atmosphere, is made up of a succession of compromises: half fairy, half mortal; half poetry and half prose. The habit and speech of no single group is allowed to dominate that of the others. The pattern of the comedies is kaleidoscopic. The focus is always changing.

This explains why some kinds of comedy lend themselves to performance before a relatively small, courtly gathering. The responses they evoke are not those of an audience that has little sense of how the people who belong to it are different from one another. That is more appropriate to the intense concentration on a single protagonist that belongs to tragedy. Instead, the grouping of the scenes, the disposition of characters and the timing of the actions within the scene all have the effect of diffusing concentration, or allowing the audience's attention to shift from scene to scene without worrying too much about the way scenes hang together. The links are insubstantial to say the least. Nobody would care to dwell too long on how Hortensio, the loyal friend of Petruchio in Act i of *The Taming of the Shrew*, became Hortensio the clumsy suitor to Bianca of Act ii of the same play; or how Hermione spent the sixteen years between Act iii and Act v of *The Winter's Tale*. Although the actions in these and other comedies unfold in broad outline in conventional terms of cause and effect, the detail that should lay open the visible mechanism by which it is done is often perfunctory and inconsistent. I see the comedies more often in spatial than in temporal terms, with actions involving different groups disposed side by side with each other, or one inside the other, touching at odd points, the one expanding for the moment whilst the other contracts to a single character watching it from the corner of the stage – Lucio in the prison in *Measure for Measure*, Ariel forever being called away from his own plot to service those of the others in *The Tempest*.

Along with this relaxing of concentration and this ease of movement from one story to another goes a failure to be absorbed utterly into the play world. The point has been made many times in recent years that in all his dramatic work Shakespeare is careful to draw attention to the highly artificial circumstances in which what is happening is happening. This is not just a matter of characters moving to the front of the stage and addressing the audience direct, totally ignorant of the convention that separates the illusory world of the stage from the real world on all three sides of it. It is a matter also of characters within the action, in dialogue and declamation, drawing attention to their histrionic identities; self-consciously composing an on-stage audience to witness another play (the 'Mousetrap' in *Hamlet*) that we see as well; or making taunting noises about the merely theatrical identity of those to whom they speak. It is noticeable, however, that the characters who do this kind of thing with the greatest aplomb tend to have a comic side to them. The greatest comedians in the tragedies are Richard III and Hamlet, and they are both keenly aware of the theatricality of their existence.

> Come, cousin, canst thou quake and change thy colour,
> Murder thy breath in middle of a word,
> And then again begin, and stop again
> As if thou were distraught and mad with terror?

That is Richard rehearsing Buckingham's tragic 'counterfeit' before they go out to do their act in front of the Lord Mayor and the people of London. Hamlet claims that his behaviour in the play scene will get him a fellowship in a cry of players, and his antic disposition is a comic act throughout. In the tragedies, the illusory character of the play world is emphasised most in those scenes which are most comic. At the great climaxes of Desdemona's murder, Lear's holding the dead Cordelia in his arms, Macbeth's terrible quarrel with his wife before he takes the knife to Duncan, there is little insistence on artifice. The audience is drawn into the scene and responds to it with horror and suspense, as each member of it might respond to a tragic event in real life.

In the comedies this degree of concentration and belief in what is happening doesn't exist. The actors make use of their actual or, in the public theatre, pretended knowledge of the people in the audience to make those people shuttle back and forth from engagement to detachment. The spectators change from being eavesdroppers to accomplices, from ignorant bystanders to know-ledgeable witnesses. And all the time they are amusedly aware of the fact that it's all a play, a game that they are sharing with the actors. Sometimes the actor has the advantage over the character, sometimes the character has the advantage over the actor. From time to time we share the advantage of one or the other and are manoeuvred into a position of laughing with the actor at the character, or with the character at the actor who is playing him. This can happen in the most unassuming parts. Take the characters of Constable Dull in *Love's Labour's Lost* and Snug the joiner in the *Dream*. Both of them are con-spicuously minor parts, and I should be surprised if they were not both played by the same actor, a good fellow who was made the butt of the playwright's and the other actors' friendly ridicule. In the preparation for the Pyramus and Thisbe play, Snug is both a character in a play and an actor of a play. So the point of Peter Quince's mockery of his Thespian virtues is pleasantly double-edged. Snug is modest about his own merits: 'Have you the lion's part written?' he asks. 'Pray you, if it be, give it me, for I am slow of study.' 'You may do it extempore', Quince replies, 'for it is nothing but roaring.' Shakespeare and the actors are looking through Snug's disguise as an actor play-ing a part, to the man he is beneath it that equips him to play it so well. Surely Snug and Dull keep turning up in some guise or another in several of the plays. I often wonder which of the Gloucestershire recruits he played in *Henry IV Part 2*. Feeble, I suppose, though Mouldy, Wart and Shadow can each lay a claim. After all, as Falstaff says, 'we have a number of shadows to fill up the muster book.'

*　　*　　*　　*　　*

Our ability to take the comedies on their own terms has been adversely affected by the way the form developed after the Elizabethans. Along with the retreat of the apron stage behind the proscenium arch went the celebratory and festive type of comedy Shakespeare had excelled at. Rules for comedy of a kind the Elizabethans had known but as often as not rejected were applied to the writing and staging of contemporary plays. From Dryden's *Marriage à la Mode* through Congreve's *The Way of the World* to Sheridan's *School for Scandal* and beyond (to the present-day Whitehall farces, in fact), comedy, whether witty or farcical, has become more and more dependent on plot; and by plot I mean the reasonable connection between one action and another that we discovered was not so very important in Shakespeare. It is what Dryden called a 'noble intrigue', derived from the late seventeenth-century respect for classical literature and, within that literature, the comic form perfected by Terence. In it the variety and looseness of the Shakespearean type gives way to concentration on a single action moving towards a conclusion which is predictable but elusive; elusive because of complications which, in the middle of the play, keep getting in the way of a straightforward, rapid movement from premise to conclusion. In Dryden's *Essay of Dramatic Poesy*, Neander describes what he considers to be an 'admirable plot' in the following terms:

> The business of it rises in every act. The second is greater than the first; the third than the second; and so forward to the fifth. There too you see, till the very last scene, new difficulties arising to obstruct the action of the play; and when the audience is brought into despair that the business can naturally be effected, then, and not before, the discovery is made.

The play Dryden has in mind is not, as it happens, a late seventeenth-century piece. It is Ben Jonson's *The Silent Woman*, first acted in 1609, roughly contemporary with such late plays of Shakespeare as *Coriolanus* and *The Winter's Tale*. Dryden is basically right in thinking that many of Jonson's' plays, and this one certainly among them, anticipated what we might call the anti-romantic pattern of later English comic drama. What is the 'business' Dryden refers to? It is the business set in motion by Sir Dauphine Eugenie in marrying his uncle, Morose, to Epicoene, the silent woman of the title. And the discovery? That is the disclosure at the end of the play that Epicoene is not a woman at all, but a boy whom Dauphine has disguised as a woman so as to get his hands on his uncle's property. The complications in the middle of the play are created by the intrigues of Truewit and Clerimont which, together with the use Epicoene makes of her new-found powers of speech, drive Morose into a corner he cannot get out of in any way but by capitulating to Dauphine's demands. In fact I am simplifying what actually happens in *The Silent Woman.* If you look at the middle scenes you will find that all sorts of things are happening which have not very much to do with the plan for getting hold of Morose's money. Sir Amorous La-Foole's dinner party and the silliness of Sir John Daw and the Collegiate Ladies, let alone the disgrace of Tom Otter, are only incidentally parts of the overall plan, Dryden's 'business'. They evolve a life of their own. Even so, the reason they are in the play in the first place is clearly to act as the brakes and levers of Dauphine's scheme. They are dominated by Dauphine just as the Anabaptists in *The Alchemist* are dominated by Subtle and Face. In each of Jonson's greatest comedies one of the rogues comes out on top, whether or not he is delivered over to justice. Volpone, Dauphine and Face are all, finally, pre-eminent in villainy in a way nobody is usually pre-eminent in anything in Shakespeare. A typical fifth act in Jonson is a hectic rush to see who can outmatch whom, repeating at breakneck pace the reversals and counter-reversals of the earlier part of the play. A typical fifth act in Shakespeare is a slow-moving series of unastonishing disclosures and reconciliations. Jonson is desperately cramming in all the business he hasn't managed to get over already. Shakespeare is spinning out the little he has left over for the end, padding out rather than cramming in.

Jonson provides a useful comparison with Shakespeare, anticipating as he does the comic form that was to supplant Shakespeare's after the Puritan interregnum. A modern admirer has written of one of his later plays, *Bartholomew Fair*, that 'the emphasis is on the narrow range of motives that actually govern men's actions, in contrast to the wide variety of warrants which they pretend to have.' This seems to me to be true of all Jonson's comedies. They are populated with two kinds of character, fools and knaves – or, in the language of his own day, gulls and sharks. The action of the play springs from the preying of the knaves upon the fools, and, when the fools are dismissed, the trial of wits amongst the knaves to find out which of them are fools in knaves' clothing and which are knaves absolute. Movement is therefore exceptionally purposive, towards a conclusion at which all the fools are banished and the knave, who has proved himself by repeated stratagems, tricks and double crossings, rises clear of the intrigue and is seen to stand at the apex of the plot, finally in control. In Shakespeare, on the other hand, this kind of arbitrary division between the characters into one classification or another does not take place, movement is meandering rather than purposive, and nothing is concluded but a series of preliminaries. The weddings at the end of *A Midsummer Night's Dream* close one phase in the lives of the couples, but open another; the end of Prospero's reign on an island in *The Tempest* is the beginning of Miranda's life in the society outside it. At the end of *Volpone*, Mosca goes to the galleys for good, and Volpone really will lie in prison until he is 'sick and lame indeed'.

Jonson's division of humanity into knaves and fools also has the effect of preventing the characters from having much of an inner life. They are what they do. It is the business of the plays to give them enough to do to enable us to know what they are. Throughout, the audience is in the position of armchair detective, its interest in character narrowed to the point at which all it is interested in is whether a character is a knave or a fool. On the surface he may present a number of differentiating features. He is often dominated by a single humour – miserliness, greed, even hatred of noise. But in the end these are indeed of the surface. What Jonson is after is the real man, the knave or fool hidden beneath the eccentric disguise. When he has brought that to the surface, where it belongs, he has done. The man is found out and the audience can go home. It is Jonson's way, then, to reduce the number of aspects of a character that we are prepared to be interested in, until all of them can be gathered under one or other of the primary classifications. A man is classified by his actions. If he goes under, he is a fool. If he stays on top, he is a knave. When only one man stands on top there is nothing more to say. The play is over.

Shakespeare isn't like this at all. We have seen that the most active people, the ones whose actions are most effective in allowing the play to happen at all, are usually very small parts. The parts that are given to Volpone and Mosca, to Subtle and Face, and the other great movers of Jonson's comedies turn up in Shakespeare's as Egeus and Don John and Frederick. We are not interested in them. The Duke in *Measure for Measure* and Prospero in *The Tempest* are exceptions that I shall have to explain when I come to deal with those plays, but by and large Shakespeare isn't very interested in finding out who is at the apex of the plot. Where Jonson externalises character and sets it to work deliberately and calculatedly, Shakespeare leaves it mysterious and mainly unobserved. Jonson is fascinated by the way characters take in other characters. The observation of method means a great deal to him. Shakespeare isn't much interested in method, which means the details of plotting, because what people are has very little to do with what they can be seen to do. He is fascinated with the way characters take in themselves, rather than other people. Taking in other people is a very simple matter involving disguises and forgeries. But beneath the disguise all kinds of subtle self-deceptions, uncertainties and psychological duplicities may be taking place which do not issue in the bold, effective action favoured by Jonson.

Jonson's disguisings are parts of a clever plan to exploit the society in which the disguiser lives. Plots are deliberate and their working out takes up the length of the play, not just a few scenes like those given over to the discomfiture of Malvolio in *Twelfth Night* or the mockery of Benedick and Beatrice in *Much Ado about Nothing*. Where in Shakespeare they do take a long time to work out, the attention of the audience is seldom applied to the links that bind the victims to the plotters as much as to the links that develop between the victims themselves. The transformations of feeling pictured in the transactions between the lovers and in the wooing of Bottom by Titania in the *Dream* are interesting enough irrespective of the tricks that brought them about. In any case there is nothing remotely criminal in what Oberon does. The idea of criminality or social exploitation rarely arises. Even a play like *The Merchant of Venice*, which reaches its climax in a court of law, has less to do with crime than *Volpone* or *The Alchemist*, because where Jonson's interest lies all in the effort to ascertain the identity of the villain and the effects of his villainy, Shakespeare's lies in a quite different direction. In his comedies, relationships between characters are not so starkly outlined. The movement from above to below, the pressure of the superior on the inferior intellect, is less important than movement from side to side, the ebb and flow of feeling between characters who are not involved in the game of acquiring such obvious and demonstrable advantages over one another.

The behaviour of Jonson's knaves and fools exposes them for what they are, but not before they in turn have exposed society for what it is: a collection of fools who would be knaves if they knew how and knaves who will be fools if they do not maintain the agility of mind and ruthless cunning that has kept them on top so far. It is therefore one of the features of Jonsonian comedy that it is satiric. The satire is not only a matter of odd *aperçus* into an absurdity here and an abuse there. It is basic and unremitting. T. S. Eliot said of Jonson that his plays are only incidentally satiric because they are only incidentally a criticism of the actual world. It is true that that is what they are. The picture of society that Jonson presents in the plays is a luridly comic caricature of rapacity and greed. But caricature depends on the existence of a world of milder forms and softer outlines; and it is expected that anyone looking at the world will acknowledge that it has something in common with the distorted picture in front of him. Jonson's world is not created *ex nihilo*. People really were rapacious and greedy, and Jonson wrote his comedies to tell them so. To that extent they have satire as their main aim in a way that Shakespeare's do not. The satire in *Love's Labour's Lost* and *Twelfth Night* is indeed incidental. In plays where it ceases to be so the tone darkens to an extent that turns comedy into something else or precludes it altogether. There is nothing very comic about *Troilus and Cressida, Timon of Athens* or *Coriolanus*.

Far from having as their main object the correction, or at least the identification, of vice, Shakespeare's comedies set out with the quite different purpose of endorsing a sentiment. We are rarely outraged by anything that happens in these plays, if we except Shylock's demand for his pound of flesh, Claudio's rejection of Hero (in *Much Ado about Nothing*), Bertram's behaviour towards Helena (in *All's Well that Ends Well*), and

Leontes' brutality towards Hermione (in *The Winter's Tale*) – and there is something unsatisfactory about all the plays in which these things happen except, perhaps, the last. Outrage is a spur to action. Shakespeare does not encourage us to be active. We are too preoccupied with the manoeuvres we have to make so as to see what is happening, to be able to afford the time to apply what we see to the world outside the play. Besides, what Shakespeare shows us more often leads to resignation than anger; there is far more folly in the world than villainy, or good sense either. But villainy and good sense manage to neutralise each other, leaving folly free to blunder into a sort of happiness. So instead of standing back and judging, Shakespeare's audience is more likely to enter into the spirit of the thing and enjoy. *What* it enjoys we shall now have to turn to – with a digression, first, into the early comedies.

2

The Comedy of Errors,
The Taming of the Shrew,
The Two Gentlemen of Verona

THE early comedies are a digression from the matter at hand because it took Shakespeare three plays apprenticeship before he hit on his distinctive comic manner. Even so, two of them are enjoyable in themselves, and the other has some claim on our attention. Let us have a look at the enjoyable ones first.

The annual revels held by the men of Gray's Inn on 28 December 1594 were not a great success. Matters got so out of hand that an 'ambassador' from the Inner Temple, who had been invited with his followers to the festivities, refused to stay and flounced out of the hall before the play he had expected to see had begun. A contemporary account of the affair takes up the story:

> After their Departure the Throngs and Tumults did some-what cease, although so much of them continued, as was able to disorder and confound any good Inventions whatsoever. In regard whereof, as also for the Sports intended were especially for the gracing of the *Templarians*, it was thought good not to offer any thing of Account, saving Dancing and Revelling with Gentlewomen; and after such Sports, a Comedy of Errors (like to *Plautus* his *Menechmus*) was played by the Players. . . . We preferred Judgments . . . against a Sorcerer or Conjuror that was supposed to be the Cause of that con-fused Inconvenience. . . . And, lastly that he had foisted a Company of base and common Fellows, to make up our Disorders with a Play of Errors and Confusions; and that Night had gained us Discredit, and itself a Nickname of Errors.

More likely a good natured effort to include the players in the convivialities than a criticism of the play. No doubt *The Comedy of Errors* would have done well enough at this sort of occasion – full of belly laughs and with at least one classical pedigree to excuse them. It was considered good enough to be revived for the same occasion ten years later in 1604. But I doubt whether it was written especially for the revels. In these early years, Shakespeare seems to have been busy making a living on the public stage. The first of the comedies that looks as if it was written for a special occasion is *Love's Labour's Lost*, and that was probably not acted until 1595. *The Comedy of Errors* is at the very least three years earlier. Against this we have to place the fact that the stage directions and the groupings of the characters both suggest that the play was designed for performance in a private hall, which would have had no gallery, and a stage divided up into three fixed locations: representing the Priory, the Courtesan's house and the house of Antipholus of Ephesus – an oddly rigid unity of place when we bear in mind the usually mobile geography of Shakespearean comedy.

The play as a whole has a 'set' quality about it. In spite of all the movement to and from the three main locations and the speed with which, after the long preamble by Aegeon, the business unfolds, we are not encouraged to move into the play world and participate in the events that are going on there. Perhaps this has something to do with the rapidity with which one action follows another. Perhaps it is in any case a feature of Shakespeare's earliest drama. Nobody gets the chance to get much involved in the perpetual slaughter of the *Henry VI* plays, and in *Titus Andronicus* Quintus's words to his brother Martius, who has just fallen into a pit, leave us in doubt as to whether we are witnessing a tragedy or a farce:

What, art thou fallen? What subtle hole is this,
Whose mouth is covered with rude-growing briers,
Upon whose leaves are drops of new-shed blood
As fresh as morning dew distill'd on flowers?
A very fatal place it seems to me.

Tragedy of blood? Or send-up of tragedy of blood? It's the same question we ask ourselves about Hammer films today. Whichever it is, whether or not the playwright had his tongue in his cheek, the effect of the speech, and of the play to which it belongs, is to set us at a distance from which we can watch one act follow another and the drama gradually acquire the shape we had predicted from the first. In both *Titus* and *The Comedy of Errors*, all the conventional tricks are used to deflect, disrupt, and delay the conclusion. But at last it comes as predicted. That was what the tricks were there for all the time.

With the bulky exception of the history plays, Shakespeare's habit at this early stage in his career seems to have been to take a stock theatrical form and produce a polished variant of it. Not surprising when you remember the circumstances in which he had to work. In the early 1590s he didn't have any share in the company (the Lord Chamberlain's Company) he wrote for. That had to wait until the Burbage brothers built the Globe in 1599. He wasn't a principal actor. Even in 1601 he is found playing the dignified but small part of the ghost in *Hamlet*. So he had to be prudent. We can tell from the accounts Philip Henslowe kept in his diary that a young writer would usually submit a skeleton plot to the head of the company, the man who had the financial responsibility, and only then would he begin to be paid, in advance, for each sheet of the play he produced. Shakespeare didn't work for Henslowe, but presumably the same sort of arrangement was made with James Burbage. If this was so it doesn't come as much of a surprise that the first of the comedies should bear so little stamp of Shakespeare's personality.

The American critic Mark Van Doren's description of the early plays is particularly suited to this one. He says that they are all 'comedies of situation, plays in which, obedient to the laws governing such matters, Shakespeare confines his interest to physical predicament – to things that happen to certain persons not because of *who* they are but because of *what* they are.' This is certainly born out by the way Shakespeare knocked together *The Comedy of Errors*. He went back to the Roman comic dramatist, Plautus, whom he would have read at Stratford Grammar School, and got hold of the plot of the two Antipholuses from a play called *The Menaechmi*. Then to make things more difficult, he added the story of the two Dromios from the same writer's *Amphitruo*. This gave him two pairs of twins who could be let loose in Ephesus in such a way as to provide an almost infinite number of permutations on the theme of mistaken identity. We are left to consider the fact that *The Comedy of Errors* is at the same time Shakespeare's shortest and his most complicatedly plotted play. As a dramatic machine, it is almost incredibly intricate. Consequently, the audience's attention is absorbed entirely in the plot. The characters are drained of psychological credibility so that the situation they find themselves in can grow more and more complex. That there is a play at all is due to a psychological impossibility, namely Antipholus of Syracuse's inability to understand the reason for all the confusion – in spite of the fact that he is in Ephesus for the express purpose of finding the twin brother whose identity would provide the solution. But Antipholus is absurdly uncomprehending: 'What I should think of this I cannot tell' is the extent of his insight into the mystery.

There is a name for comic drama that subordinates credibility of character to rapidity of movement. It is farce. *The Comedy of Errors* is, technically, a farce in so far as characters in it do not so much relate as collide with one another. Transactions between them are frequently physical. They have the effect of setting and keeping in motion a progressively complicating and potentially violent plot. Typical props are a rope, a chain and a barred door. Servants are repeatedly beaten, the doctor is cuffed and his beard singed, and one of the protagonists is arrested, bound, and thrown into 'a dark and devilish vault'. The last act shows us women fleeing an innocuous Antipholus of Syracuse who is then himself bemused into flight and persuaded to enter 'with drawn sword'. The pattern is one of unfortunate collisions and tantalising evasions. Everything depends on the unlikely double premise that the two Antipholuses and the two Dromios will not meet each other; and the greater part of Shakespeare's energy goes into making credible the fact that they do not do this until Act v. The audience is held in suspense by the split-second timing, awaiting the inevitable exposure, but having it put off time after time in ways that make it look as if when it does come it will be even more explosive than it was expected to be before. Eric Bentley has written about farce in the silent cinema in these terms: 'The speeding-up of movement in the typical silent-movie farces had a definite psychological and moral effect, namely, of making actions seem abstract and automatic when in life they would be concrete and subject to free will.' Shakespeare's plotting and speeding up of the pace of the narrative in *The Comedy of Errors* is the equivalent of the speeding up of the film in the Keystone movies or René Clair's adaptation of Labiche's *The Italian Straw Hat.*

This is all very entertaining, but it is an essentially trivial form of theatre, manipulating the responses of the audience at their most rudimentary level, which is one of expectation, suspense, relief. All theatre does this, but in its more serious moments it uses what it predicts the audience's response will be to organise and communicate ideas, the expression of sentiment, complex modes of thinking and feeling. Farce evades responsibility for this. It lowers the threshold of the writer's ambitions and encourages responses of the kind I have described, as ends in themselves. Farce produces laughter at the same level as melodrama produces terror. In each case the sensation is cut off from anything approximating to reality. A situation is 'given' from which the play takes off, at each point moving further and further beyond the circumstances that gave rise to it. The audience is discouraged from tracing events to their source One unusual event owes its existence to another. The frail and narrow base upon which the edifice of intrigue gyrates and expands is usually, as it is here, scarcely credible, highly artificial – just acceptable enough to get the whole thing going. I have not found anything in *The Comedy of Errors* that goes beyond this. The farce is skilfully contrived, the bemusement of the characters is funny, and so is the anger and fear they display. With our superior knowledge we can recognise that neither of these emotions is at all appropriate to the true state of affairs. The hiatus between what is the case and what the characters believe is the case produces farce and laughter, nothing more nor less.

I have to insist on this because it is a view that is not shared by many modern critics and editors of the play. Some make very much more ambitious claims. E. M. W. Tillyard, for example, believes that Clair's *Belles de Nuit* is a more appropriate comparison piece than his *Italian Straw Hat* because *The Comedy of Errors* goes 'beyond farce'. It belongs to a group of plays that, like most farces, begin in ordinary life but 'they then turn ordinary life into something fantastic and remote from life; and then somehow they seem to rejoin life, but at a different point, so that, instead of making us feel what an amusing holiday from life this is, they cause us to exclaim, "Oh but life after all can be as strange as all this." ' I cannot believe this is so. Still less can I believe that 'in transcending farce, *The Comedy of Errors* raises the question of what is the norm of reality'. This would describe the Shakespeare of 1596, not the Shakespeare of 1591. Tillyard has mistaken the impression the play actually makes in performance by substituting the sympathetic response appropriate to romance for the very much more detached and 'callous' response appropriate to pure farce.

It's easy to see why he made the mistake. Shakespeare's later comedies are very much preoccupied with such matters as Tillyard discovers here. Furthermore the play is 'framed' by the account of Aegeon's shipwreck, a highly romantic story lifted from John Gower's translation of *Apollonius of Tyre*, the same source Shakespeare was to use again for the most romantic play he ever wrote, *Pericles, Prince of Tyre*. Some of the romance sentiment seeps into the play proper. Ephesus, where the scene is laid, was celebrated for magic arts, and Shakespeare deliberately changed Plautus's Epidamnus to Ephesus. Again, the behaviour of Antipholus of Syracuse in Ephesus is very strange, and there are quite open references to illusion and transformation scattered throughout the play. In III, ii, for example, Antipholus of Syracuse wonders why Luciana labours to make his soul 'wander in an unknown field':

Are you a god? Would you create me new?
Transform me, then, and to your pow'r I'll yield.

None of this is conclusive. Aegeon and the Duke firmly absent themselves from the story that unfolds in the middle acts, and further references to the sea and ships – usually poignant with mystery and strangeness in Shakespeare – are strictly practical and pointedly unromantic. The wooing scene between Antipholus of Syracuse and Luciana is thoroughly untypical of the play in almost every respect – in its substance, its lyrical manner and its quatrain form. It is soon over and nothing like it happens again. Antipholus is soon enough pleased to be escaping from Ephesus without Luciana in tow. The scene is a brief lyrical interlude in a play otherwise notably devoid of lyricism. Quite the contrary. We are encouraged to respond to what happens in a manner that is automatic and Pavlovian. Antipholus wanders in illusions so that we may laugh, not ponder the nature of illusion itself. We don't have the time.

The Comedy of Errors is a farce. It has us respond to an intricately assembled combination of suspenseful but abstract occurrences. The Apollonian romance is stuck to the beginning and end to enable us to take in a lot of information we need to know before the play can properly get started. It is also a pleasantly romantic story in its own right; and it is a guarantee that no harm is likely to come of the confusions we are allowed to witness, since we know all the time that Aegeon exists in the wings as a *deus ex machina* who will be trundled on-stage when things get near enough to bursting point. The play does not transcend farce – it uses farce to achieve ends that are proper to farce – surprise, suspense, laughter. And a very good farce it is too.

★   ★   ★   ★   ★

The Comedy of Errors is almost unique among Shakespeare's works in being pure farce (apart from the fanciful frame). It is also unique in being entirely unconcerned with the romance and absurdity of courtship (with the minor exception of the scene between Antipholus of Syracuse and Luciana). The nearest Shakespeare ever came to it again was seven or eight years later in *The Merry Wives of Windsor*, and even there the wooing of Anne Page by Master Fenton is more spaciously developed than the wooing that goes on in the earlier play. In what was probably Shakespeare's next play, *The Taming of the Shrew*, the 'dominant' plot is equally though not similarly farcical. It is not similar for two reasons. One, laughter is produced by the straightforward development of a simple and single comic situation. Though the aggravation of the initial circumstance – Petruchio's determination to tame his wife – is as absurd and extreme as it was in *The Comedy of Errors*, the circumstance itself is uncomplicated and boldly outlined. There is no need for the kind of prologue offered to us by Aegeon in the previous comedy. Second, the circumstances that create the comedy take the form of a relationship between the sexes, during and immediately after courtship.

Adriana in *The Comedy of Errors* was a shrew, but that was all she was and the part she played was in any case relatively small. Kate is much more than that, and Petruchio's feeling for her, at times, is very much more interesting and engaging than was Antipholus of Syracuse's for Adriana. These changes in the subject and form of the play make a change also in the kind of laughter it produces.

In *The Comedy of Errors*, because we were in possession of information none of the characters acquired until the end of the play, we laughed *at* the characters. In *The Taming of the Shrew*, laughter *at* the characters still predominates, but it is tempered from time to time with an amusement we derive from entering *into* the situation of Petruchio's courtship of Kate. I think something of this can be felt in iv, v, where the two of them are on the road to Padua to visit Kate's father shortly after the marriage. Kate's willingness to agree with (or is it humour?) Petruchio about the sun's or moon's position in the sky, and her mocking address to Vincentio as a 'gentle mistress', betray a hint of pleased capitulation to her husband's demands which suggests that she understands the game she is supposed to be playing and proposes to play it well. She goes further than Petruchio requires she should and, in spite of a hint of impatience in her tone, we feel she is getting some satisfaction out of 'overdoing' it, moving through the game to a position from which she can mock at Petruchio – from the sidelines. Or maybe he is on the sidelines too, so that they have a mocking detachment in common. The fact that the play can throw up questions like these – making us wonder about the degree of complicity of the two main characters in the action to which they belong – is a sign that more is going on, at something other than a superficial level, than was the case in *The Comedy of Errors*. There is evidence of it elsewhere as well. In i, ii, it is often difficult to tell at what point Petruchio starts and stops jesting with his friend Hortensio about his interest in Katherine. In ii, i, as elsewhere, the attitude of Katherine and Bianca to the marriage market seems to be contrasted, to Kate's advantage.

In each of these cases we find ourselves participating and discriminating, searching for the correct position from which to look at things, in a way we never did in *The Comedy of Errors*. There is a different degree of involvement in the action from what had been there before. But it is intermittent, and where it exists it is rather crude, operating in respect of very simple responses from the characters. Most of the time it is not encouraged and so it does not exist at all. Here also, many commentators have tried to mature Shakespeare too early, arguing the case for a deliberate and subtle psychological study of Kate throughout the play. The most slapstick actions are interpreted as manifestations of a complex inner condition.

Again E. M. W. Tillyard is one of the guilty parties. Kate, he believes, possesses profound inner contradictions, and Petruchio a 'delicacy and perceptiveness of feeling' which will surprise many theatregoers who have been used to watching him chasing Kate around the stage and bullying his servants, cook and tailor. Take the middle of II, i, the courting scene. It is surely a very subtle move on Petruchio's part to pretend to an arrangement with his betrothed 'that she shall still be curst in company' so as to save her face before the others 'if she should change her tune and accept him quietly'. Not so. Surely the reason Petruchio is doing this is to place the others in a position of misplaced confidence which will be crudely comic to the audience. Shakespeare is going along with the conventionally farcical procedure of placing the audience in a superior position to the characters – except Petruchio and Kate, which does make something of a difference, but not the difference Tillyard assumes is there. He is converting a convenience of the plotting into a subtle play of character. Ingenious, but out of step with the intentions of the play as a whole. The same applies to his comments on the opening of the same scene. Here Kate is discovered with Bianca asking about her lovers rather as Nerissa is to ask Portia in *The Merchant of Venice*:

> Of all thy suitors here I charge thee tell
> Whom thou lov'st best. See thou dissemble not.

Tillyard's explanation is that Kate is obliquely disclosing to the audience a very genuine interest in men which lurks half confessed beneath her apparent disdain. There may be something in this. It is true that the characterisation of Kate does fill out the more one rereads the play. But surely the main reason for the scene is much more obvious. It is there to inform us, prior to Lucentio's arrival, that Bianca's feelings are unattached, that she is in love with neither Hortensio nor Gremio. In other words it serves the second plot more than the first. Kate is the means whereby Bianca's feelings are revealed to us, not the principal character in a scene given over to the explanation of her own personality.

What of the second plot itself? Where the first is derived from a widely known folk-theme and issues in farce, this one hails from the Classico-Italianate comedy that Shakespeare was to use so often in the future. It is an adaptation of George Gascoigne's translation of the Italian novella *I Suppositi* (*Supposes*) and is the first example in the comedies of a second action developing concurrently with the principal one. Notably, the usual balance is reversed. Farce takes pride of place over courtly romance.

As a romance there is little to be said for or against it, except that it interacts very skilfully with the Petruchio–Kate plot; and it provides Shakespeare with an opportunity (in v, i – Vincentio and the pedant) to rework the scene in *The Comedy of Errors* (III, i) where Antipholus of Ephesus is locked out of his house. Shakespeare was often reluctant to let go of an indifferent joke. The same thing happens with the bed trick in *Measure for Measure*, which turns up again immediately after in *All's Well that Ends Well*. It also reveals Shakespeare assuming an easy, though somewhat naïve, confidence in a variety of types of blank verse; the lyrical tone of some of Lucentio's addresses is very thin, nothing like as assured as the rumbustious stuff Petruchio treats the tailor to in IV, iii. As a matter of fact, the only distinguished lyrical verse in the play is not found in either of the main plots, but in the frame.

This, the Induction, is something of a problem. It existed in an earlier play called *The Taming of a Shrew* which was certainly produced in 1594 (and probably earlier too), and which may be an earlier version, by Shakespeare, of *The Shrew* that we are looking at now. In our *Shrew* it ambles along very pleasantly for a couple of scenes and then disappears, apart from a single perfunctory re-emergence at the end of I, i. In *A Shrew*, it appeared more often and there was an epilogue. In spite of some ingenious justifications by scholars, I think we must conclude that our Induction is unnecessary. Unnecessary, but splendid – both for the vivid prose that Christopher Sly speaks, and

for verse like this, in which the lord and servants convince him
of his wealth and status:

> Wilt thou have music? Hark! Apollo plays,
> And twenty caged nightingales do sing.
> Or wilt thou sleep? We'll have thee to a couch
> Softer and sweeter than the lustful bed
> On purpose trimm'd up for Semiramis. . . .
>
> Dost thou love pictures? We will fetch thee straight
> Adonis painted by a running brook,
> And Cytherea all in sedges hid,
> Which seem to move and wanton with her breath
> Even as the waving sedges play wi'th'wind.

It is one of the first fruits of Shakespeare's study of the Roman
poet Ovid, whose descriptions of the metamorphoses of gods
and men were to haunt him throughout his life. It is Ovid
dressed out in the eloquent periods of his greatest English imitator,
Christopher Marlowe, who had used just such language six or
seven years earlier to express Tamburlaine's love of beauty and
its incarnation in his wife Zenocrate. And it is a preliminary
sketch for the more elaborate counterpoint of the voices of
Lorenzo and Jessica in the fifth act of *The Merchant of
Venice*.

The *matter* of the Induction also does more to anticipate the
later comedies than do any of the scenes from the play itself.
When the verbal music is over, Sly is not sure whether he is
awake or dreaming, awaking from or into a dream:

> Am I a lord and have I such a lady?

he asks,

> Or do I dream? Or have I dream'd till now?
> I do not sleep. I see, I hear, I speak;
> I smell sweet savours, and I feel soft things.
> Upon my life, I am a lord indeed.

And he proceeds to witness the play – the play we also witness,
but which includes him both as dreamer and as part of the
collective dream. At the end of the play he might have said,
with Bottom in *A Midsummer Night's Dream*, that he had

'dream'd a most rare dream'. Indeed he did say something like that in *A Shrew*. But in the play we have, nothing is made of it. Sly disappears, and the audience settles down to watch a lively knockabout that casts no doubt upon what is real and what is dramatic spectacle. The promise of the Induction is left unrealised.

Shakespeare was to do nothing to remedy this state of affairs in his next comedy, which has what I should suppose is a unique attribute amongst his works: it is not enjoyable. It is merely a preview of better things to come. *The Taming of the Shrew*, with all its bluster and lop-sidedness, is by far the best of the early comedies – the one with most life and least pretensions.

* * * * *

The Comedy of Errors and *The Taming of the Shrew* are neither of them distinctively Shakespearean in tone or movement. Where we catch a glimpse of the mature playwright, it does not stay for long: a single speech by Luciana, one or two speeches by Petruchio and Kate, above all the Induction to *The Taming of the Shrew*. By way of contrast the entire structure of *The Two Gentlemen of Verona* is in many ways typical of the structure of Shakespearean comedy. Romantic love is at the very centre of the plot; tyrannical fathers try to repress the generosity and passion of youth; one character revives his drooping spirits in a pastoral, forest setting; another disguises herself as a boy and woos her lover's new mistress in the form of his page. The bickering of Petruchio and Kate was a crude sketch for the 'set of wit well play'd' between Benedick and Beatrice in *Much Ado about Nothing*. Here, in *The Two Gentlemen of Verona*, there are try-outs for Claudio's treatment of Hero in the same play and Bertram's of Helena in *All's Well that Ends Well*; there is a preview of the Arden setting in *As You Like It*, complete with a forerunner of the Duke's speech there about the books in the running brooks and sermons in stones; and there is a lengthy practice-run for Viola/Cesario's wooing of Olivia on Orsino's behalf in *Twelfth Night*. This list by no means exhausts the anticipations of later scenes and devices. Almost every scene can be paralleled right down to Valentine's rope ladder, which finds its way into *Romeo and Juliet* a couple of years later.

We need not stop at details of the plot. The characters also are the earliest examples of types we find Shakespeare using over and over again in the later comedies. Silvia is the artful, but reasonable woman of the world; Julia the spirited, ardent lover who invariably proves to be a much more positive character than the man she loves. Proteus especially, but Valentine also, is the immature but accomplished young man who begins his discovery of the world by discovering his love for a rich, pretty, and much-too-good-for-him young girl.

In spite of all this, *The Two Gentlemen of Verona* is a pale shadow of the plays it precedes, bearing the same relation to the mature comedies as an architect's plan bears to a house. It has everything we come to expect of a Shakespeare comedy except the atmosphere, the air and light, the density of texture and glowing colour that invests scene, character and sentiment alike. The setting is not, like the setting of some of the other plays, Venetian; but if it were it would be a Venice painted by Carpaccio as compared with a somewhat later Venice painted by Giorgione. Shakespeare seems to have been blind to everything in his story which does not support its structure and define its shape.

Dr Johnson, as usual, had an explanation. 'In this play' he wrote 'there is a strange mixture of knowledge and ignorance, of care and negligence. . . . The reason for all this confusion seems to be, that Shakespeare took his story from a novel which he sometimes followed, and sometimes forsook, sometimes remembered, and sometimes forgot.' Johnson is referring to the absurdities in the plot, of which there are even more examples in this play than in the other comedies – taking the trouble to sail from Verona to Milan, for instance. But this sort of thing doesn't bother us so much. We tend to worry more about the artificiality of the psychological complexions of the characters – the sheer stupidity of Valentine, the absurdly abrupt reconciliation in the forest immediately after Proteus has tried to rape Silvia before Valentine's very eyes. Shakespeare's comic heroes are usually a bit on the weedy side, but we have difficulty in envisaging any of the others handing his mistress over to a neurotic rapist, however incompetent he is at the job. This is the crowning silliness of a play much given to silliness of one kind or another. The Duke's (or is it Emperor's?) 'discovery' of Valentine's plan to elope with Silvia is just one more spectacular example. It is as if Macbeth asked Duncan how much wine and wassail it would need to put his grooms out and how many knives they had. Even when we make due allowance for the fact that *The Two Gentlemen of Verona* is a comedy, our patience is sorely tried.

On this matter I think Tillyard is right. He believes that what went wrong was Shakespeare's handling of the main source. This was the story of Felix and Felismena in Jorge de Montemayor's *Diana Enamorada*, which was entirely concerned with the nature of love between the sexes. The plot was a variant of the eternal triangle. There was no fourth party to complicate things, no friend of 'Proteus' to cross the romance with the second theme of friendship. Shakespeare, by precipitating Valentine into the story, and attaching a great deal of importance to the role he plays in it, created a situation in which he had to humanise and clarify Proteus's subsequent emotional conflict – torn between the claims of love and friendship. Instead, he backed down. He refused to allow Proteus a character at all, which rendered his behaviour contemptible and ridiculous. Why he did this we shall never know. The Renaissance was fascinated by the rival claims of love and friendship. Shakespeare himself was much concerned with the behaviour of a treacherous friend in matters of courtship – in the sonnets (though Heaven knows *The Two Gentlemen of Verona* doesn't sound like the expression of an inner compulsion to lay a private ghost). All we can say is that in a bungled way Shakespeare presents us with all the prominent features of his comic method, but throws them together in a way that renders them absurd or distasteful. At the same time atmosphere – romantic engagement and willingness to piece out the poet's imperfections with our thoughts – is totally lacking. (Incidentally the tedious prevalence of duologue may have something to do with this. *The Two Gentlemen of Verona* has the distinction of being the least evidently populated of Shakespeare's plays).

The verse is correspondingly unremarkable – indulging, where it is not more drably workaday than anywhere else in Shakespeare (including *The Comedy of Errors*), a vein of studied eloquence which affects neither body nor wit. It has a slight artificial lyric grace. For example at II, vii Julia expresses her love for Proteus to Lucetta in the following terms (Lucetta has already given Julia a metaphor to play with – quenching the fire of love):

> The more thou dam'st it up, the more it burns.
> The current that with gentle murmur glides,
> Thou know'st being stopp'd, impatiently doth rage;
> But when his fair course is not hindered,
> He makes sweet music with th'enamell'd stones,
> Giving a gentle kiss to every sedge
> He overtaketh in his pilgrimage;
> And so by many winding nooks he strays,
> With willing sport, to the wild ocean.
> Then let me go. . . .

and so she goes on, pointing out each detail of the comparison of love to a stream flowing out to the sea. The sedges here are not Marlovian, as they were in the Induction to *The Taming of the Shrew*. They are more precious and decorative, more clearly a part of an elaborate but not very penetrating argument. They belong to the earlier Elizabethan prose writers, John Lyly in particular, whose *Euphues and his England* is chock full of this kind of ornate comparison and syntactic elegance. Valentine's pathetic outcry on hearing of his banishment from Silvia in III, i ('And why not death, rather than living torment?') is another example of linguistic artifice, this time working through paradox and antithetical parallelism. Proteus's reflections on Silvia's picture at IV, ii, are typical of the affected style of the play at its least pedestrian.

Each of these three speeches displays a kind of eloquence that will be satirised in the heroes and heroines of the later plays – in Olivia in *Twelfth Night*, for example. There it will be used both as a target for mockery and, suitably qualified with wit and the correct degree of self-consciousness, a touchstone of right sentiment. Here it is simply the honest expression of adolescent love. Shakespeare is enjoying the changes he can ring on it, which are not many, and so it has little corrective intent, merely persuading the audience to take note of its happy self-indulgence, along with the removal of the sentiment it is supposed to define and celebrate.

Shakespeare's progress as a comic writer from this point until *Twelfth Night* took the form of a reassembly of the properties we have discovered in *The Two Gentlemen of Verona*, varying their distribution and deepening their tones. Two things were necessary. First, of course, an increase in professional skill, the acquisition of a greater command over the techniques at his disposal. Second, something more difficult to pin down. A different perspective on the action of the plays was required. Shakespeare needed to find a way of jolting his audience into a different state of mind, into a new kind of activity. He needed the instruments of enchantment to soften outlines, which were still hard and intractable; to deepen the response to behaviour, which was still mechanical; and to make acceptable shifts of allegiance and changes of emotional fortune which, at this stage, still look artificial and contrived. The first of these prerequisites took time. As Shakespeare developed as a dramatist he steadily extended the range of his technical resources. The second he achieved at a single step. Unfortunately he did so in a play, *Love's Labour's Lost*, that is the most topical and therefore in long stretches the most ephemeral he ever wrote. What he achieved in this play has been darkly obscured for later generations by the riddle in which it is so irritatingly wrapped.

3

Love's Labour's Lost

At the close of *Henry VI Part 3*, the Yorkist monarchy is secure and Edward of York, now Edward IV of England, feels strong enough to dispatch his old antagonist Margaret of Anjou to France:

> Away with her, and waft her hence to France.
> And now what rests but that we spend the time
> With stately triumphs, mirthful comic shows,
> Such as befits the pleasure of the court?

What comic shows did he have in mind to grace the occasion of his victory? Jesting and foolery, perhaps. But they would have been available every day. This is not every day. It is an occasion to be celebrated, like a wedding or a visit from an important foreign dignitary. The mirthful show referred to need not be just the comic pendant to a stately triumph, contrasting markedly with the dignity of what preceded it. Instead it might have been the comic equivalent of the triumph, equally befitting the nobility of the court and the good taste of its members. Could Shakespeare, at the time he was writing *Henry VI Part 3* (probably about 1590) have provided such an entertainment? *The Comedy of Errors* and *The Taming of the Shrew* are decidedly student and citizen fare. *The Two Gentlemen of Verona* would have come nearest, thought it can rarely be described as mirthful, and it is hardly a 'show' – except in the obvious sense that it is a play written for the stage. None of these plays would have been absolutely appropriate. Though their protagonists have steadily climbed from the merchant to the courtly classes, the audience they have in mind is undoubtedly a public one, in which the nobility was not conspicuous. So in 1590, and up to three years later, Shakespeare could not have obliged Edward.

But with his next comedy, *Love's Labour's Lost*, he might have had better luck. This play is in all likelihood the first Shakespeare wrote for a select and aristocratic audience. F. P. Wilson guessed that the Quarto is a revision of an earlier version acted at Titchfield, the Earl of Southampton's house in Hampshire. Shakespeare seems to have been cultivating the young Earl's friendship and patronage in the early 1590s, *Love's Labour's Lost* was probably written during the plague year of 1593–4 when the London theatres were closed, and Titchfield was a place where courtly shows must have taken place often: Queen Elizabeth had visited it at least twice, on her progresses of 1569 and 1591, and would have expected to be royally entertained. Cut off from the social life of the capital, Southampton and his friends would have been anxious for plays and festivities, and Shakespeare would have been eager to provide them. At about the same time he was writing his Ovidian narrative poems, *Venus and Adonis* and *The Rape of Lucrece*, both of which are dedicated to Southampton. It looks as if from about 1593 to 1596 – with plays like *Love's Labour's Lost*, *A Midsummer Night's Dream* and *Romeo and Juliet*, and with the elegant narrative poems already mentioned – Shakespeare was making a determined effort to break into the circle of the nobility, to create a market for sophisticated and intricately patterned literary *jeux d'esprit* of a kind that would have appealed to young blades like Southampton, Essex and their peers. Later, in 1609, Southampton appears to have entertained the new Queen with a production of *Love's Labour's Lost* at his house in London. He might have recollected its success more than a decade earlier at Titchfield.

As an aristocratic entertainment I believe it inaugurates a long line of such comic plays written specifically for an occasion – festive, seasonal, or celebratory of a court event. *A Midsummer Night's Dream* was almost certainly a wedding entertainment. *Twelfth Night* might have been enacted at Whitehall in 1601 as a court celebration of the last twelve days of Christmas. *The Tempest* was produced at Whitehall in 1611 and again at Whitehall in 1613. In other words, after *Love's Labour's Lost* a number of Shakespeare's comedies are known to have been either written or adapted as festive entertainments, probably of the kind Edward IV requested at the end of *Henry VI Part 3*.

What difference does it make? I have tried to answer this question in my introduction, where I point out that the main difference lies in the changed relation between play and audience, and players and audience. This was for two reasons: the audience would be much smaller than at the Theatre or the Curtain (or the Globe after 1599); and it would also be more homogeneous, at least more knowledgeable of itself, of the people whom it comprised, than the public theatre. This in turn would make a difference not merely to the way in which a performance would be felt as an occasion, but also to the way the playwright handled his material, which was so often, and had been once or twice before (in *The Two Gentlemen of Verona* and in the Lucentio–Bianca plot of *The Taming of the Shrew*), the behaviour of noblemen and young gentlemen. It makes a great deal of difference whether a writer does or does not compose *for* the class he is writing *about*. In writing about gentlemen to gentlemen much can be taken for granted, a great deal can be left unsaid. The writer can assume a tactful intimacy with his audience which would have been out of place in writing about the same social classes for the public theatre.

Looking at the plays at the present time this appears to be a mixed blessing. For there is no class today which precisely answers to the description of the company Shakespeare's earls and dukes kept, and the interests and gossip of the groups that come nearest to them have to do with quite other subjects. What is tactful reticence for one generation is wilful obscurity for another. Ease of discourse and 'leaving the rest unsaid' leaves all too much to be said by modern editors, solving linguistic riddles in a barrage of footnotes that threaten to sink the play. There is plenty of opportunity for this in *Love's Labour's Lost*. The King of Navarre's Academy has been interpreted as an ironic analogue to Raleigh's School of Night (referred to by name at IV, iii), and the matter involving Sir Nathaniel, Don Armado and Holofernes may be a satire on the Martin Marprelate controversy, Moth's puns on purses and pennies being intelligible only in their application to Thomas Nashe's pamphlet *Pierce Penilesse* which has an oblique bearing on the business. Set within the satiric treatment of these subjects is a plethora of mocking attacks on such topical literary affectations as Inkhornism (the irresponsible invention of new words from classical sources) Euphuism (imitation of the decorative style of John Lyly) and the use of Spanish importations to increase the vocabulary. None of these is likely to set the modern theatre alight. Taken together, they are the penalty we have to pay for Shakespeare's first foray into the cultural milieu of the Elizabethan aristocracy.

There are compensating virtues, which are inseparable from the intimate association of the play's concerns with those of its courtly audience. For the first time, in *Love's Labour's Lost*, the audience are invited to become involved in the play as festive celebrants, in a way that has been best described by C. L. Barber in his book on *Shakespeare's Festive Comedy*. Professor Barber believes that in what he calls the 'idyllic' comedies, release is expressed by making the experience of the play like that of a revel – for actors and audience alike. The 'holiday humour' that Rosalind refers to in *As You Like It* (IV, i) 'is often abetted by directly staging pastimes, dances, songs, masques, plays *ex tempore* etc. But the fundamental method is to shape the loose narrative so that "events" put its persons in the position of festive celebrants; if they do not seek holiday it happens to them.' And so 'the process of translating festive experience into drama involved extending the sort of awareness traditionally associated with holiday, and also becoming conscious of holiday itself in a new way'. This goes some way to explain how Shakespeare achieved the new perspective on the action of the play, the involvement of the audience in what was happening on stage, that I have insisted was lacking in the early comedies. It is the 'extension of awareness', in Barber's words, that Shakespeare managed to produce for the first time in this play.

Even in those early comedies, Shakespeare appears to have wanted to do something different, to place his audience in a less rigidly detached position than the action of the play demanded. Two of them have oddities of shape: the romance form of *The Comedy of Errors*, the lapsed Induction of *The Taming of the Shrew*. In each case the principal events are surrounded or at any rate inaugurated either by events of a different kind or by events expressed in a different sort of language. But in the context of the experience of the play as a whole, the 'framing' devices don't work. Far from providing an invitation to the audience to release themselves from their customary 'set' ways of looking at things, they tend to have the opposite effect, trapping them in a habit of detachment appropriate to farce and therefore successful only in a very conventional way. Shakespeare did not relinquish his interest in these framing devices, but he never again used them so directly or clumsily as he did here. Briefly, what he had done so far was to make the frame out of what should have been the picture, and the picture out of what should have been the frame. What was outside should have been inside, and *vice versa*. But Shakespeare was too busy playing with the intricacies of Plautan and Italianate plots to see that the right things were in the wrong positions. *Love's Labour's Lost* is the first play in which the imbalance is corrected. The narrative is much looser and simpler than it was in *The Comedy of Errors*, *The Taming of the Shrew* or *The Two Gentlemen of Verona*. The fashioning of an aristocratic entertainment has persuaded Shakespeare to use the plot as a mere 'surround' to the body of the play, which is made up of conversational, romantic, festive material that, until now, had taken decidedly second place to the intrigue.

The plot is in two parts. In one part the King and his courtiers fall in love with the Princess of France and her ladies. In the other, Don Armado struggles with Costard for the prize of Jaquenetta. It doesn't amount to very much. The complicated transactions of *The Comedy of Errors* or of the Lucentio–Bianca affair in *The Taming of the Shrew* are nowhere to be found. All the actual plotting is more in the nature of a game than a serious effort to control events. No one behaves like the suitors of the *Shrew* or like Proteus when he discloses to the King Valentine's plan to elope with Silvia in *The Two Gentlemen of Verona*. All the intrigue revolves around Costard's inability to send the right letter to the right person, and the consequences of that are very rapidly dispatched. Indeed the plot is so flimsy that even with a great deal of stalling and delay it is more or less over by the opening of Act v. Costard has his Jaquenetta; and the King and his courtiers have fallen in love, discovered their love to one another, and decided to close the academy. All that remains to be done is to tell the ladies and celebrate the outcome. As it happens their wooing does not end like an old play. But that is not because of a development of the intrigue; it is simply because it is announced that the King of France, who has been off-stage throughout, has died, and the ladies must go home. Which means that Act v, which is almost as long as all of the first four acts put together, has very little work to do. The plot is over only a little more than half-way through the play. What is to be done with the rest of it?

The ladies have to make their replies to the lords' professions of love. But that can scarcely take an hour and more. The announcement of the King of France's death has to be made. But that, together with the Princess's response, takes less than a quarter of an hour. The rest is almost entirely composed of dance, song and pageantry – the masque of the Muscovites, the pageant of the Nine Worthies, and the exquisite Winter and Spring songs that end the play. None of these advances the action, for there is no action to advance. Instead they pick up suggestions from the earlier scenes and convert the play into a celebration, a sort of display during which the narrative peters out and the characters appear in guises not their own or as stage audiences imperceptibly merging with the real audience in the hall. I should be surprised if the mockery with which the King and his young men greet Holofernes as Judas and Moth as Hercules was not echoed by the other courtiers and their retinue who comprised the audience. The gap between stage and auditorium has closed, as it has almost closed many times before – not just in Act v, but in Act iv too, in the long 'sonnet' scene in which Longaville discovers Dumain, the King discovers Longaville, Berowne discovers the King and we have discovered Berowne, long before Costard brings in what he thinks is Don Armado's letter and gives the game away. Here again we have a little play within a play. We are inevitably drawn to the conclusion that over two-thirds of the play is show, performance, display; and that what is left over is more a dramatised series of preparations for such displays than an intrigue in its own right. Plotting has little to do with the merits of the play, or with our response to it.

The best way of describing *Love's Labour's Lost* is as a medley set within the progressively dissolving framework of a play. Inside the shell of the play we find the pert wit of Moth, the clowning of Costard, the satirical parody of Sir Nathaniel, Don Armado and Holofernes, the 'operatic' sequence of discoveries involving the four young men, the masque, the pageant, the dancing and the song – all enlivened and 'pointed' by the sketchy goings-on of the characters, who exist more to do that than to draw attention to themselves in their own right. This variety of formal arrangement is echoed in the patterns of the verse that expresses it. There is a greater range of styles in this play than in any other comedy before it. Apart from the blank verse and the songs there are at least four varieties of couplet, quatrains, sonnets and lyric measures. All of this is contained in a dramatic structure which I have described as progressively dissolving because of its accelerating tendency to fall apart into multiple instances of display; and I have said that it does this because it is at once a type of and a substitute for those courtly entertainments in which the audience itself, and not its stage substitutes, took part. Here the audience has it both ways. It doesn't have to take part, but it receives every encouragement to do so. The behaviour of the Navarrese is the pattern of their own. They have only, therefore, to join in with them at the appropriate times to enjoy the festive occasion where the world of the stage joins the world of the audience, or where the world of the audience joins the world of the stage. By this time, the distinction has been blurred so much that it is difficult to tell which way round to put it.

The form of dramatised medley, with incorporated pageants and displays, fulfils two main requirements of the time. It makes the audience willing to respond to the events as an intimate group, allowing Shakespeare to count on their sympathy – and, incidentally, their sharing his gentle critique of manners and types of artifice. This sympathy broadens outwards from a shared response to people and their conduct, to a *rapport* with the 'atmosphere' they combine to produce. One senses this even in the setting of the play. For the first time in Shakespeare, all the events take place in a setting that seems utterly appropriate to them, within which they cohere, link with one another, affect one another with little sense of strain or contrivance. Both topographically and in terms of 'mood' it all seems of a piece. Though there are only a few explicit references, we cannot imagine the play without its geography of the 'curious knotted garden' where Armado saw Jaquenetta misbehaving with Costard, the coppice where the ladies are discovered shooting deer, or the thicket of sycamores where Boyet heard the Muscovites preparing. The crazy park is a much more substantial place than Ephesus, Padua, or even Petruchio's house near Verona. The opportunities it affords for odd contacts between the Lords, the Curate, the Spaniard and their servants and the ladies encamped just beyond it, make it possible for us to plot the relationships between its parts and ponder the associations its details call to mind.

Also the play of character, even detached from the plot that usually expresses it, is much more subtle and less mechanical than hitherto. The courtship of Berowne and Rosaline improves on the earlier courtship of Proteus and Silvia or Petruchio and Kate, as much as it is later improved upon in its turn by Benedick's courtship of Beatrice in *Much Ado about Nothing*. We can see in what the improvement consists by comparing Proteus on the power of love in *The Two Gentlemen of Verona* with Berowne on the same subject here. This is Proteus in *The Two Gentlemen of Verona* I, iii:

Thus have I shunn'd the fire for fear of burning,
And drench'd me in the sea, where I am drown'd.
I fear'd to show my father Julia's letter,
Lest he should take exceptions to my love;
And with the vantage of mine own excuse
Hath he excepted most against my love.
O, how this spring of love resembleth
The uncertain glory of an April day,
Which now shows all the beauty of the sun,
And by and by a cloud takes all away!

He is rationalising his transfer of feeling from Julia to Silvia, and he does it very prettily and unexceptionably down to the apostrophe 'O how this spring of love'. Here the language starts to take off and hovers on the brink of the expression of real passion. Premature, however. The quatrain closes just as the speech is getting off the ground, rather as the quatrains of the early sonnets tend to fizzle out in the middle, and die at the couplet. Proteus's love isn't given the chance to grow. It withers on a rhyme. Both Juliet, and Lysander (in *A Midsummer Night's Dream*) are given speeches with a similar emphasis on the transitoriness of love; but it is not the context only which gives to their speeches, despite their brevity, a faster pulse and a greater urgency than is displayed here in *The Two Gentlemen of Verona*.

Berowne's attitude to love is the opposite of Proteus's – and that of many of the young men in the early plays. Far from dulling his senses to everything else and making him a slave to his quest for the lady, he finds that love is an energising and vital force, enlarging his mind and sharpening his wits. Book-learning in the academy is all very well, but love – that is something different and more satisfying altogether:

> But love, first learned in a lady's eyes,
> Lives not alone immured in the brain,
> But with the motion of all elements
> Courses as swift as thought in every power,
> And gives to every power a double power,
> Above their functions and their offices.
> It adds a precious seeing to the eye:
> A lover's eyes will gaze an eagle blind.
> A lover's ear will hear the lowest sound,
> When the suspicious head of theft is stopp'd.
> Love's feeling is more soft and sensible
> Than are the tender horns of cockled snails;
> Love's tongue proves dainty Bacchus gross in taste.
> For valour is not Love a Hercules,
> Still climbing trees in the Hesperides?
> Subtle as Sphinx; as sweet and musical
> As bright Apollo's lute, strung with his hair.
> And when Love speaks, the voice of all the gods
> Make heaven drowsy with the harmony.

And so on. The speech possesses all the sweetness and delicacy of Proteus's lines (by the way, those snails have appeared before, in *Venus and Adonis*) but with an added power. As Berowne says later in the same speech, they sparkle with the right Promethean fire. They remind us of those speeches by the Lord and his men in the Induction to *The Taming of the Shrew*, and they have the same origin, in Tamburlaine's speech on beauty – 'What is beauty, saith my suff'rings then'. The hyperbole of the lines on Apollo are superbly Marlovian, and the whole manages to sustain the note of enraptured lyricism over a spacious twenty or thirty lines. It isn't fashionable nowadays to praise Shakespeare for the sheer splendour and spaciousness of his lyric gift; but we shall get the emphasis of these early romantic plays quite wrong if we overlook it.

Eloquence counts for a great deal in these lines, but not for everything. We also have to notice where the speech fits in Berowne's developing awareness of the nature of love, and as we do so we notice too an obliquity and subtlety gained from the position it occupies within this development. At the end of the third act Berowne, realising he was in love with Rosaline, had considered the situation to be absurd. Love was no more than a 'wimpled, whining, purblind, wayward boy' and women like German clocks, 'Still a-repairing, ever out of frame,/And never going right.' There was something in this view. Not everything, but it was part of the truth. What he says in IV, iii is also a part of the truth. Love is part rapture, part humiliation. It is also part affectation, as Rosaline points out to him in V, ii, when she corrects his ascent into French whilst he is confessing that his love-making shall henceforth be expressed 'in russet yeas and honest kersey noes'. Even at the very end of the play the staying power of Berowne's love is in doubt, and he is packed off to visit the sick and talk with groaning wretches for a twelvemonth, before he comes to a decision about whether he will marry Rosaline or not. His speeches must stand the test of time and be subdued to a more even tenor and a less exalted expectation.

Berowne's change of attitude is a striking example of a change that comes over all the lords. This has been variously described by critics who have their own ideas about what constitutes the proper behaviour of young men placed in such a position. The best description I have come across is the one made by John Dixon Hunt in his essay, 'Grace, Art and the Neglect of Time in *Love's Labour's Lost*'. He takes the view that what the lords acquire through their disclosure to themselves of their love for the French ladies is 'grace', in the sense Longaville intends in his sonnet to Maria:

My vow was earthly, thou a heavenly love;
Thy grace being gain'd cures all disgrace in me.

Berowne uses the word in his address to the ladies at V, ii:

We to ourselves prove false,
By being once false forever to be true
To those that make us both – fair ladies, you;
And even that falsehood, in itself a sin,
Thus purifies itself and turns to grace.

This is grace as Baldassare Castiglione understood it in his hand-book for courtiers *Il Cortegiano, The Courtier* (very popular with the Elizabethans; it would be surprising if Shakespeare had not read it and been impressed by it). There, Cardinal Bembo explains how divine love is revealed to men and women through physical beauty, especially beauty of face, the fine proportions of which should be reproduced in the conduct or courtesy of the individual who possesses them. The lords' decision to forswear the company of members of the opposite sex has cut them off from grace. This is made obvious by the awkward manner in which the King receives the ladies into the outer limits of his court. It is probably made *visibly* obvious by the costumes worn by the King and his party, no doubt sombre and academic, until they resume their customary gaiety after the masque of the Muscovites. At the close the lords rededicate themselves to the natural passage of time by breaking their vows to study for an arbitrary period of one year. In doing so they commit themselves to the orderly sequence of the months and years in which grace can be sought and courtesy practised. Therefore the satire of the middle acts 'insists upon the precious and precarious balance necessary in all arts (those of living as much as those of the court or stage) between what is formal and calculated and what is spontaneous and partakes of life'. This goes some way to explain the presence in the play of Armado, Holofernes and their companions. They too, like the lords, endeavour to construct an ideal order (of words rather than of actions or behaviour) at the expense of the real, imperfect world they have to live in; whereas it is clear that such an order can emerge only from natural imperfection – it cannot be set up in artificial contradiction to it.

So the change in Berowne's attitude to love is of a piece with all the lords' changing attitudes to what is expected of them in their search for 'grace', which they had at first supposed they would obtain through the fame that would 'have register'd upon our brazen tombs' as a result of their studies at the little academe. But his love for Rosaline is more fervently expressed in the speech I have quoted than is anything the other lords express anywhere else in the play. Of course it has to be judged within the context of the bafflement of the courtiers and the corrections of the ladies, as well as within the context of its own origins and aims. The imagery in which it is expressed also has to be placed alongside the gently critical hints offered to the audience in respect of its appropriateness – its appropriateness to Berowne's imperfect grasp of the demands of love. Though love is not blind, as he is traditionally held to be in the figure of Cupid and as, at different times, Speed, Thurio and Julia supposed he was in *The Two Gentlemen of Verona*, nevertheless he is invariably associated with the eye. Silvia believed that Proteus, again in *The Two Gentlemen of Verona*, worshipped shadows and adored false shapes, but it is not until *Love's Labour's Lost* that the association of love and the sense of sight is so emphatically made. In Berowne's speech the stress falls on 'the prompting eyes/Of beauty's tutors' and only then on the transmission of love from the eyes in which it originates and the eyes which respond to it, to all the organs of sense and feeling. We talk of falling in love at first sight. No one but Shakespeare, however, has taken the phrase so literally. Shakespeare's lovers look at each other more interestedly and more lingeringly than anyone else's. Boyet thought that all Berowne's senses were locked in his eye, that all senses to that sense did make their repair; and when Berowne tries to press his suit to Rosaline, even after the ladies have heard the news of the King of France's death, he expresses the view that love is

> Form'd by the eye, and therefore, like the eye,
> Full of strange shapes, of habits, and of forms,
> Varying in subjects as the eye doth roll.
> To every varied object in his glance.

With this hint of the subjective delusion of love, its power to distort and render familiar things strange and strange things familiar, we move into the territory of *A Midsummer Night's Dream*. We must pause before we enter it, picking up the threads of what we have discovered so far.

Love's Labour's Lost, we have found, represents the opening phase of Shakespeare's mature romantic comedy. It is obviously an aristocratic entertainment, and its impact is in part somewhat restricted by its being so self-consciously an aristocratic entertainment. Many of the preoccupations of the play are society, enclave, preoccupations, and this narrows its scope considerably. In later comedies Shakespeare will often make use of the festive, open form arrived at here, and extend it – possibly as a result of increased self-confidence, and audacity too – to meet the requirements of a larger, public and more varied audience. He will also retain and increase his insight into the quiddity and psychological intricacies of romantic love, with a corresponding development of verbal and theatrical resource. As a result his next play is a comic masterpiece for all time, one of his works that is always popular and always bewitching. Let us pass on now to *A Midsummer Night's Dream.*

4

A Midsummer Night's Dream

A Midsummer Night's Dream, like *Love's Labour's Lost*, may have been an entertainment for the nobility; more precisely, an entertainment to celebrate a wedding. The evidence from outside the play to support this view is sparse and inconclusive, but I should have thought the internal evidence was clear. The theme of the play is marriage. Three couples are married at the end of it, and one more, Oberon and Titania, have represented another version of the married state throughout. Theseus and Hippolyta are ideal lovers awaiting their wedding with the proper degree of impatience and ceremony; and it has been suggested that since they are given so small a part in the story – nothing happens to them – they may represent a flattering stage substitute for the betrothed in honour of whose marriage the play was first performed. There are plenty of parts for small boys who would have lived in the household where the celebrations were being held. What could be more suitable for children to speak than the monosyllables of Peaseblossom, Cobweb, Moth and Mustardseed at III, i? And, of course, there is a repeated insistence on festive revels by members of all three groups on-stage: the nobles, the fairies, and the mechanicals. Altogether, the evidence from inside the play points to the fact that it was originally a wedding entertainment.

In some respects the play is formally similar to *Love's Labour's Lost* too. It is a narrative of the trials and tribulations of a group of lovers; the setting in which the play of wit and fancy is enacted is insisted upon even more than was the case there; and again the action is to all intents and purposes complete by the end of the fourth act, leaving the fifth to take the form of a set of festive entertainments. This last is the most important link between the two plays because it makes clear, at the same time, what is so *dis*similar in the effects they produce. The relative proportions of plot and what I have called 'display' are very different. To begin with, the fifth act is nothing like as long as it was in *Love's Labour's Lost*, and the preparations for the festivities (by the mechanicals and, in a less direct way, the fairies) have been proceeding since Act I. They are not sprung upon us as an impromptu affair as they were by the King and his company or by Don Armado and his friends. In other words the *Dream* again has a plot at its centre. We may not attach the same importance to it as we did in *The Comedy of Errors* or *The Two Gentlemen of Verona*, but there can be no getting away from the fact that it is there and has to be attended to.

Furthermore there is not one plot, or two – as in the first three acts of *Love's Labour's Lost* – but four: those involving Theseus and Hippolyta; Oberon and Titania; Bottom and the mechanicals; and the four lovers. They are by no means distinct. At first glance Theseus and Hippolyta seem to be somewhat separate from the rest, though we must remember that their wedding is the reason for the presence of both fairies and mechanicals in the wood near Athens, and it is Theseus's command that has driven the lovers there. Theseus and Titania, and Oberon and Hippolyta have known each other before. The perplexities of the lovers are the direct result of Oberon's inter-ference (through Puck), as is Titania's grotesque indiscretion with Bottom. Connections are made between the most unlikely mem-bers of all four plots. This is all the more surprising when we consider that the characters in them do not seem to belong to the same worlds. In *Love's Labour's Lost* differences in station and profession among the characters contributed to the creation of a uniform play-world – that of the crazy park of Navarre in which people had distinct and definite relations to one another. They all fitted into place. In *A Midsummer Night's Dream* this is not so. The play of Pyramus and Thisbe is not the only 'alien' substance. Its assimilation to the world of the play as a whole is paralleled by the assimilation of the fairy world to the mortal world; if assimilation is the right word, and if Shakespeare really intended that it should be achieved – a matter we shall have to turn to later.

What has happened is that the flat narrative-conversational plane of the earlier play has been replaced by a series of mobile perspectives. By this I mean that instead of shuttling between the two positions of witnessing a play and participating in an entertainment, the audience is invited to look through or across one 'plane' of action to another beyond, before or to the side of it. The obliquity of the play has much to do with the ease with which it makes the audience's perceptions narrow and expand to include or exclude aspects of one world where their main concern is with those of another. The best way of explaining this is by a diagram:

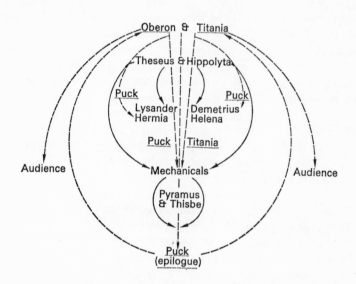

This is a flattened-out representation of the main lines of force in *A Midsummer Night's Dream*. I don't mean it to be taken too seriously. All I want it to do is to make clear the way in which the activities of the fairies cut across and get entangled with those of the mortals (to make this as clear as possible I have used a dotted line for the fairies and a continuous one for the mortals). Whenever we are concerned with either the fairies or the mortals – certainly in Acts II–IV – we cannot prevent particles of the world we are not concerned with gliding into the picture. And not as background only, but as a kind of shadow, a bright shadow, that falls across the lens through which we are looking. This goes some way to account for the perceptual elasticity we experience in watching *A Midsummer Night's Dream*. Now let us see what happens when we set the plan in motion.

As it stands, the plan shows Oberon and Titania at the outer limits of the drama. They appear to be in control of what happens and to be responsible for the way the audience takes it in. This needs some explanation, since they do not actually start things off. They do not present us with an unquestionably final outer frame from the outset, as Christopher Sly looks as if he will do in *The Taming of the Shrew*. In fact they are the last major characters to appear, and they act out their roles in a setting (the wood) which itself seems to be 'held' within the action initiated by Theseus (or Egeus to be precise).

Also the characters of Oberon and Titania are not impressive at first sight. They do not look like the best people to be in control of affairs. Compare their debut with that of Theseus and Hippolyta. The Athenian pair are first on stage. Theseus is impatient for the wedding night and complains of the slowness with which the old moon wanes before the nuptial hour will come. His desires linger 'Like to a stepdame or a dowager/Long withering out a young man's revenue'. But Hippolyta is a calming influence:

> Four days will quickly steep themselves in night;
> Four nights will quickly dream away the time;
> And then the moon, like to a silver bow
> New-bent in heaven, shall behold the night
> Of our solemnities.

Theseus is reconciled to four days' restraint and puts his impatience behind him. Melancholy is fit only for funerals. It is time to awake the pert and nimble spirit of youth with pageantry and merriment:

> Hippolyta, I woo'd thee with my sword,
> And won thy love doing thee injuries;
> But I will wed thee in another key,
> With pomp, with triumph, and with revelling.

There is a time and a place for everything. Oberon and Titania, however, do not think so. They enter at II, i, not together, like Theseus and Hippolyta, but the one at one door and the other at another. Obviously they are in a pet:

Oberon: Ill met by moonlight, proud Titania.
Titania: What, jealous Oberon! Fairy skip hence;
I have forsworn his bed and company.
Oberon: Tarry, rash wanton; am not I thy lord?
Titania: Then I must be thy lady; but . . .

It is all very unappetising, a fit of pique, an ill-tempered squabble
– with both parties straining unsuccessfully for the kind of
dignity that is supposed to come from drawing yourself up to
your full height and taking long breaths through distended
nostrils. But it is not their appearance and tone alone that is
ridiculous. What are we to make of their claim that as a result
of their quarrel all nature is diseased, rivers have overborne
their continents and the seasons have been set at sixes and sevens,
frost in spring and ice in summer – a whole progeny of evils
that has come from their dissension? Theseus and Hippolyta
haven't noticed any of this, and it hasn't prevented Lysander
from singing at Hermia's window in the light of a moon that has
made none of the court rheumatic or distempered, and that
Hippolyta sees as conducting its usual stately progress through
the heavens. The fairies seem to be both irresponsible and ego-
centric, not at all the right people to exercise control over nature,
not adult folk like the Duke of Athens and the Queen of the
Amazons.

That is the impression we get from this initial contrast between
the two couples. But as the action continues and the interactions
between the mortal and the fairy worlds develop the relation
between the control exercised by the fairies and the control
exercised by Theseus undergoes a number of transformations.
After I, i, Theseus and Hippolyta disappear and do not return
until IV, i. In the meantime their happiness has become an
object of concern to the fairies. We hear of them all the time
as being included in the scope of the fairy power. Then, with
their reappearance in Act IV, they show themselves to be unfamiliar with the powers the fairies have at their disposal – the
powers which, it transpires, get Theseus out of a very tricky
situation. For if it had not been for Oberon the Duke would
have had no alternative but to force Hermia into a marriage
of convenience with Demetrius or to send her to a nunnery or
to execute her, souring both Lysander and Helena in the process.

Not a very good start to the wedding celebrations, and not a very good end to a comedy. But Oberon gives Puck his orders and after all the mistakes and complications, harmony is achieved – by supernatural, not natural means. Finally the sleeping lovers are encircled in the charmed world of the fairies, which accounts for the outer frame of the retrospective diagram.

The outer frame of the court looks as if it encloses the experience of the 'wood outside Athens' of II, i – IV, i. That is the way it appears from Act I looking towards Act II. Really, the experience of the wood curves back from a point almost at the end of the play and encloses what had at first seemed to be its mortal frame. We understand this only gradually, as we move into and (perhaps) out of the dream. So what is this magical experience the fairies preside over? And how far are we able to get outside of it so as to include it within the total experience of watching the play? Let us start by entering the wood and seeing what happens to us when we get there.

Seeing is not as simple as you would expect it to be, in these surroundings. We have some difficulty in making out just what is going on. Not only our sense of sight, but all our other senses are persistently strained. There is continual mention of defective sensory organs producing mistaken impressions or the belief that things are present that are not present and that what is present is an illusion. Simultaneously we have to make more use of all our senses than we are used to, and we have to distrust the evidence of even the most highly developed of our senses. As Hermia says at III, ii:

> Dark night, that from the eye his function takes,
> The ear more quick of apprehension makes;
> Wherein it doth impair the seeing sense,
> It pays the hearing double recompense.

This is not just a matter of nervous reactions to the dark. Or if it is, we shall have to take it more seriously than we have done hitherto. It is Theseus, at V, i, who dismisses the matter in such common-sense terms. In the night, he says, imagining some fear, 'How easy is a bush suppos'd a bear?' But he is standing, or he thinks he is, outside the world of the wood. Inside it things are different. All the time we, in the audience, have to rectify the

imperfections of the dramatic illusion with our working imagination, and in doing so we find ourselves deprived of any stable
centre from which perception can issue without irregularity or
distortion. Nothing fits together to compose a homogeneous,
manipulable, interpretable world.

First, there is the vexed question of the sizes of the fairies.
These had appeared earlier in John Lyly's comedies, and Oberon
had been the presenter of Robert Greene's *James IV* (*c* 1590).
Shakespeare seems to have been the first to stress their tiny
stature. They had always been played by children – six children
drew the coach of the Queen of the Fairies in the Woodstock
entertainment of 1575, and Lyly's plays were written for the
Children of the Chapel. But in Shakespeare they are minuscule.
In his Queen Mab speech in *Romeo and Juliet* (I, iv), Mercutio
had said that the fairies' midwife is 'no bigger than an agate
stone/On the forefinger of an alderman'; and here, in *A Midsummer Night's Dream*, the first Fairy is supposed to go about
hanging pearls in cowslips' ears and Bottom is supposed to be
able to wipe his nose on Cobweb. But how can Bottom blow his
nose on the Cobweb we see on the stage? And if Titania and
Oberon are on the same scale as the rest, how can Theseus and
Hippolyta have had affairs with them? They must have been
very uncomfortable. We have to keep making allowances for
what we see and what we hear. Bottom is wooed by Titania as
an eligible young woman, but Cobweb and the other fairies
serve her as a diminutive sprite. The sizes of the fairies grow
and diminish in the mind's eye. But in front of our physical eye
they stay the same – i.e. those of the boy actors who play them on
the stage.

Then there is the way the action of the play fans out in space
and time. The fairies have come to Athens from India, Oberon
is used to sitting on promontories by the ocean, and the fairy
attendants are ubiquitous in the extreme. Oberon's vision extends
to encompass stars shooting madly from their spheres and contracts to see Cupid's arrow flying between the cold moon and
the earth and piercing a little western flower 'Before milk-white,
now purple with love's wound.' Whilst Oberon and Titania
bring to the action a suggestion of enormous vistas traversed in
the past, the lovers bring to it a constricting present where each
of them is ensnared in a maze of pathways leading back and

forth, round and round through the wood. The lovers live for the moment, switching partners as rapidly as they change locations. Titania is able to lose herself in her reverie of the distant past when she and the mother of the changeling boy gossiped in the spiced Indian air by night and sat by the sea-shore watching sailing boats drift across the water. In the middle of the hectic present the past opens up, much as it did in the Nurse's recollections in *Romeo and Juliet*. We in the audience sense the weird concurrence of past and present, of the confined scene and the spacious outer world in which it is set.

Last, there are odd discrepancies in the information we are given. This goes beyond the 'double' size of the fairies. There are also the peculiarly wide and narrow powers Puck seems to possess. He can put a girdle round about the earth in forty minutes, but he can't find Demetrius although he spends the whole night wandering through the wood looking for him. Again, one piece of information that should tally with another fails to do so. Puck has two sets of powers to correspond with the two things he has to do, but they don't fit together. Each of them seems to belong to a different person.

These are all strains placed on the audience's capacity to assemble the information it receives into an intelligible order. They are reinforced by the play of imagery, especially in the central action in the wood – along with *Romeo and Juliet* the first fully worked-out example of Shakespeare's use of reiterative imagery for thematic purposes. Mainly the images are of eyes, water and moonlight. Helena's speech about the relationship between the eye and the mind, and love and judgement at i, i, is reminiscent of Berowne's in *Love's Labour's Lost* (iv, iii):

> Things base and vile, holding no quantity,
> Love can transpose to form and dignity.
> Love looks not with the eyes, but with the mind;
> And therefore is wing'd Cupid painted blind.
> Nor hath love's mind of any judgment taste;
> Wings and no eyes figure unheedy haste;

But it is not true that love is blind. Instead, the eye is made the servant of the mind, its vision distorted as if it were itself twisted and mis-shapen. It is notable that the lovers' vision is distorted and transformed by grossly physical means: herbs crushed into

their eyes, streaked with the juice of wet flowers played upon
by moonlight – a moonlight in which every part of the wood
is steeped. The moon is traditionally the image of change and
inconstancy. Here its virtue enters the bodies of the lovers as
it is reflected in the sap that 'sinks in the apple of their eye'.

A combination of the appeal to the eye and the drenching
imagery of moonlight and water affects the audience's apprehen-
sion of the action as if its own interpreting eye were streaked
with a distorting liquid film. I have often pondered how I should
stage this play. The effect one would like to produce might be
achieved by placing an enormous sheet of glass with drops of
water running down it between the actors and the audience. That
would be strictly impracticable, of course, but it conveys the
impression I have in mind. Both physical and conceptual shapes
have to be broken down, rendered fluid and molten. Here again
the imagery that produces this effect is reinforced by the deliberate confusion of sense impressions. The audience's legiti-
mate expectations are frustrated. In III, i, Peter Quince tells
Flute that Bottom has gone but to see a noise that he heard
– a theatrical synaesthesia that is typical of the way sensations are manipulated in this play. In II, i, Helena finds that
'Apollo flies and Daphne holds the chase': the normal relations
between the sexes adumbrated in the Greek myth have been
reversed, and so rendered abnormal. What Tillyard said happens
in *The Comedy of Errors* really does happen here. As Professor
Barber puts it, 'The teeming metamorphoses which we encounter
are placed in a medium and in a moment where the perceived
structure of the outer world breaks down, where the body and
its environment interpenetrate in unaccustomed ways, so that
the seeming separateness and stability of identity is lost.' The
situation in which Antipholus of Syracuse found himself has
been internalised. What in the earlier play was a trick of the
plot is here a condition of the mind and senses.

This is the dream from which the lovers have to awaken.
Not just the lovers, however. We also have shared the dream.
We too must awake. For the hypnotic power of the language,
combined with the mysterious groupings of characters on the
stage, has seduced us into sharing in the experience of the lovers
– a *dérèglement des sens* through which a final harmony might
be achieved outside the limits of the dream. The status of the

dream remains equivocal. In I, i, Lysander had believed that if there were any sympathy in choice it was 'Swift as a shadow, short as any *dream*'. But the quality and effectiveness of the dream is not to be measured in terms of length or brevity. When Demetrius realises he is in love with Helena in IV, i, he cannot understand how it has happened: 'I wot not by what power,/But by some power it is.' His speech precedes the judgement made by the lovers on the experience of the wood as they emerge from it at the end of the same scene. Each of them is baffled and uncomprehending, but each also testifies to the power Demetrius had recognised earlier:

> *Demetrius*: These things seems small and undistinguishable,
> Like far-off mountains turned into clouds.
> *Hermia*: Methinks I see these things with parted eye,
> When everything seems double.
> *Helena*:   So methinks;
> And I have found Demetrius like a jewel,
> Mine own and not mine own.
> *Demetrius*:   Are you sure
> That we are awake? It seems to me
> That yet we sleep, we dream.

At first the experience is set back at a distance, its solidity and power rendered insubstantial in the same way as mountains seem to turn into cloud. Then, step by step, it moves into the middle distance, then into the foreground – 'yet we sleep'. The irruption of the 'real' world into the dream, as the lovers move away from the wood that produced it, is muted by the way it appears. Theseus's arrival with a hunting party is dream-like, with its musical confusion of hounds and horns. Hippolyta says she never heard 'so musical a discord, such sweet thunder'. Also, Bottom's waking is delayed. He has had 'a dream past the wit of man to say what dream it was'; and the way he goes about describing it makes it quite clear that its synaesthesic power is by no means evaporated.

Act V opens with Theseus and Hippolyta again apparently in control of the situation, though this time they disagree about how to approach it. Their opinion on what has happened to the young people conflicts. Theseus takes up the man-of-the-world point of view: it is 'More strange than true', a matter of 'shaping fantasies', 'airy nothings', mere 'tricks' of the imagination. For Hippolyta, on the contrary, there has been a transfiguration. Look at Demetrius and Helena. Only yesterday, who would have thought it possible they would be reconciled and betrothed to each other? The story of the night 'grows to something of great constancy'. The emphasis falls on the power of the dream to spill over into day-time living, to exercise a persistent influence on the conduct of the dreamer. The rest of the act presents a state of affairs in which each of these views is overlaid by the other. No certain conclusion is arrived at. All we are given is what the shape of the play as a whole suggests. Is the dream contained in the waking, or the waking in the dream? We are not told, in so many words. Nevertheless, there are hints thrown up by the way the play ends. They offer little comfort to those who would make of Shakespeare a level-headed realist who knew what was real and what wasn't when the crunch came. It was Dr Johnson who refuted Berkeley by kicking a stone to prove it was there. Shakespeare doesn't kick. He lifts a finger to touch a dream. And the dream resists.

Some of the incidents seem to belie this, to suggest that the dream can be tidied away and 'placed' in a scheme of things underpinned by quite a different outlook on experience. The play of Pyramus and Thisbe, for example, which takes up a large part of the last act, doesn't merely parody the story of Romeo and Juliet that Shakespeare had dealt with in the play before this one. The way Theseus describes it to Philostrate makes it sound very like the experience in the wood. In both cases the audience has to 'find the concord of this discord'. The 'hot ice and wondrous strange snow' that he observes in it take us back to the 'hoary-headed frosts' that fell 'in the fresh lap of the crimson rose' for Titania in II, i. In other words it turns out to be a comic parody of the preceding in which the wonder and strangeness of love are indeed laid siege to by war, death and sickness, as Lysander said they were from the beginning. The mechanicals' presentation of the play is also 'nothing impaired, but all disordered' with Bottom seeing a voice and hearing Thisbe's face. In such ways are the tergiversations of the lovers reduced to inconsequence. When the play of Pyramus and Thisbe is over, Theseus steps forward to stage-manage its sequel. To Bottom's request he answers that there shall be no epilogue, but they will all dance a Bergomask. This done, Bottom and the mechanicals exeunt, and the Duke himself provides an epilogue, apparently not merely to the play-within-a-play but also to the whole play of which it is a part.

It is here that we begin to wonder again who is really in control. Theseus ordered the lovers to bed with the warning that ''tis almost fairy time'. He continues:

> I fear we shall out-sleep the coming morn,
> As much as we this night have overwatch'd.
> This palpable-gross play hath well beguil'd
> The heavy gait of night.

Night will spill over into day as much as day has already encroached upon night. If we look at the last scenes of the play again we shall find that this is even more true than Theseus has disclosed. The day that should have elapsed between the discovery of the lovers (at the same time as Puck hears the morning lark) and the celebration of the wedding (close on midnight) has somehow failed to appear. When Bottom rouses himself, immediately after the waking of the lovers, he spends a whole day – whilst Quince and the others are trying to find him – speaking twenty or so lines about his most rare vision. In terms of speech-time on the stage, day is decidedly inferior to night. Then the Duke refers to a palpable-gross play. The immediate reference is clearly to Peter Quince's play. Is it not also a mocking reference to the play *A Midsummer Night's Dream*, which has also beguiled the heavy gait of night? If this is so, and I think it is, Theseus is speaking a double epilogue; but prematurely in the case of the play *in toto*. For it does not finish here, as he anticipates. It is continued by the fairies who round off the action with a song and a dance. In the end, Theseus does not preside. Even his epilogue is rendered void, since when Oberon and Titania and their train have left the stage, Puck remains, and offers an epilogue of his own: and this really does close the play.

Let us conclude our excursion through *A Midsummer Night's Dream* by having a look at Puck's epilogue. He addresses the audience as follows:

> If we shadows have offended,
> Think but this, and all is mended,

That you have but slumb'red here
While these visions did appear.
And this weak and idle theme,
No more yielding but a dream,
****
So, good night unto you all.
Give me your hands, if we be friends,
And Robin shall restore amends.

At least two of the references are ambiguous. Who are 'we shadows'? All the actors who have taken part in the play? If so, the plea is conventional, a typical apology for taking up too much of the audience's time. But it might equally well refer to the fairies, the really shadowy creatures, who have only a minute or two before left the stage and who have all along been associated with visions and slumber. In this case the plea is unconventional, an invitation to the audience to bestow credibility on fairy powers – with the emphasis falling on the 'but' slumbered and 'but' a dream. Then, what are 'these visions'? If just the fairies, it is made certain that the earlier 'shadows' must also have been the fairies, thus rendering the first plea definitely unconventional. On the other hand if the visions include all the beings represented on the stage, this plea is itself rendered unconventional. For what we are being told is that mortal and fairy existences are equally visionary: of course they are, because both are represented by mere actors. However we construe Puck's references in the epilogue, if we are consistent we have to agree that the fairies seen in the play are no more illusory than the mortals. If we are inconsistent, we are in any case in agreement with the conclusions of the play and there is no more to be said.

Then Puck offers his hands to the audience. A gesture of the real to the real or the illusory to the illusory? Or is that distinction tenable any longer? In wishing the audience his conventional good night, he beckons them out to the world of love and imagination presided over by the fairies – a world of 'fierce vexation' and of the power of harmony; where things befall preposterously, but end in the gentle concord Theseus mentioned at iv, i. Either way, the life of the imagination is conceived as at once capricious and healing, deranging and, finally, conducive to harmony – just as it presented itself to our straining perceptions in the wood, and, indirectly, to our comprehension of the pattern of healed relationships it brought about at daybreak. It is in this sense that the dream lasts and is all-powerful. As we gaze into its depths we see reflected back at us the greater dream in which all of us subsist. We are, like actors in the play, shadows that imagination amends; and if this is the silliest stuff that ever we heard, we had better leave *A Midsummer Night's Dream* alone, arguing with Hippolyta that we are aweary of this moon. Would he would change.

5

The Merchant of Venice

It happened that whilst I was writing these chapters on Shakespearean comedy, the Royal Shakespeare Company opened its
1971 season with a production of *The Merchant of Venice*.
Terry Hands, who directed it, decided to play one of the games
I was talking about. Before the first night he gave it out that
there would only be one chair on stage, suggesting that his
would be a production stripped of superfluities and reduced to
its bare essentials. Then, as the audience filed into the theatre,
they faced an uncurtained stage resplendent with precious objects,
stately galleons dipping and rising upon a map of the oceans of
the world, the whole blazing with golden light and sparkling as if
studded with jewels. It is true that there was only one chair – the
one in the trial scene. But the audience's expectations were given
a jolt. Why did he do it? Why, to start with, should the audience
allow itself to be persuaded that this, of all Shakespeare's plays,
could sensibly be produced on a stage as empty as Mr Hands
pretended his was going to be? We have shattered the fantasy
that the Elizabethan stage was bare and costumeless. One glance
down Philip Henslowe's accounts in 1598 is enough to do that:
Phaeton's chariot, a tree of golden apples, a chain of dragons,
etc. But there is a lingering puritanism in favour of bare boards
and the power of the poetry to set the scene and keep it in the
mind's eye for the space of three hours. Mr Hands was playing on
it, quite legitimately, to surprise his audience into entering the
real, romantic Venice (and later Belmont) that had so often been
denied them in the past.

He also did something surprising with Shylock. One of the
critics of the production (Irving Wardle in *The Times*) wrote of
it that 'It is the case with this play that while its form is that of a
fairy tale its characters are open to realistic analysis; but that as
soon as such analysis begins it appears that none is sympathetic
enough to deserve a place in any fairy tale.' Shylock, more than

anyone else, is open to realistic analysis. So, if you are going to insist on the romantic, fairy-tale quality of the play, you have to do something about him. You have to make him smaller somehow, which is what Mr Hands did. As another critic (Harold Hobson) put it, 'Emrys Jones' Shylock is a comic prancing Jew without dignity or distinction of any kind.' It is at this point that I part company with the Royal Shakespeare. It seems to me that what a production of *The Merchant of Venice* must attempt is to do justice to both sides of the equation Mr Wardle sketched out. On the one hand, the fairy-tale – complete with opulent Venice and ethereal Belmont; on the other, the outsize figure of Shylock, poised to shatter the romance out of which he grows by appealing at the same time to our fear of the unknown and our respect for a common humanity. It is a tall order – one that Shakespeare himself might not have completely satisfied. It is also what the play demands, a fact that is supported, I think, by a glance at its stage history.

Shylock was always a central figure in the play. Ask any schoolchild who is the merchant of Venice and he will as likely as not reply, Shylock. Shakespeare's contemporaries seem to have had the same idea. It was entered with the Stationer's Register in 1598 as 'a book of the *Merchant of Venice*, or otherwise called the *Jew of Venice*'. When it was revised in 1701 (the first recorded performance since 1605) in George Granville's version, it held the stage for forty years as *The Jew of Venice*. There is a second point of interest about this. As far as we can tell, Shylock was always played as a comic character. In the 1701 revival he was played by Thomas Dogget, the low comedian. Now, one of the bores of writing about *The Merchant of Venice* is that it is virtually impossible not to write, at the same time, about the history of anti-semitism in this country. There weren't many Jews in Elizabethan London. They were readmitted here, after their expulsion by Edward I in the thirteenth century, by Cromwell, and would not have been a familiar sight until well into the eighteenth century. So they could be put to work very well as stage bogeymen both in the Elizabethan and Restoration periods. Nobody thinks twice about abusing a name that doesn't have a person behind it. It was not until the age of sentiment had arrived that Shylock's non-comic potentialities received any emphasis. This means that in looking at the representation of

Shylock we must bear in mind two things: the foreignness of Jews in the Elizabethan period; and the wide, but not comprehensive, humanity of Shakespeare. There is a third complication too. Around the time Shakespeare was writing *The Merchant of Venice* a Portuguese Jew, Roderigo Lopez, physician to Queen Elizabeth, was being tried and executed for plotting the murder of the Queen and the pretender to the throne of Portugal. This would presumably have affected Shakespeare's portrait of the Jew – there is a passage, in iv, i, in which Shylock is compared with a wolf (lupus).

To resume our stage history. When *The Merchant of Venice* was revived (in Shakespeare's not Granville's, version) in 1741, Charles Macklin played Shylock as a tragic character. He has remained so, for the most part, ever since. Edmund Kean made his reputation as Shylock in 1814, and Kean's reputation was for highly coloured tragic acting. Henry Irving's Shylock in 1879 was one of his most powerfully moving parts. What we have seen, then, is that from the very beginning Shylock appears to have usurped the centre of the stage, and from the middle of the eighteenth century he has done so as a tragic protagonist. It is useless, but interesting, to speculate on whether Richard Burbage, who was the main actor in Shakespeare's company by 1595–6, played him in the original production, and – if so – how. In recent productions, however, Shylock has often been removed from the centre with the object of dismissing what is commonly felt to be a sentimental, romantic view of his stature and function in the play, with the result that he has been 'integrated' into its dominating romance pattern. So the central pivot of *The Merchant of Venice* has shifted to a position mid-way between Venice and Belmont, represented by their most important inhabitants, Bassanio and Portia. This places Shylock a little to the side of one half of the play, acting as an instrument whereby the forward movement of the romance is conventionally impeded. He attracts interest in himself only on the margin.

In my view this reading is both historically improbable and directly contrary to the experience of most people who have read the play. There is a grain of truth in it, though. Shylock certainly does act as such an impediment in a comedy, which, like so many of Shakespeare's, contains enormous tragic potential. The movement of Shakespearian comedy is usually from uncertainty and dangerous confusion through to a happy resolution at the close. The initial difficulty springs most often from an artificial blockage that gets in the way of the mainstream of the action. Youthful lovers are threatened by unreasonable and extreme prohibitions imposed by the old or the powerful or the wealthy. But, as Berowne says in *Love's Labour's Lost*, 'Young blood doth not obey an old decree.' And the plays are full of these. In *Love's Labour's Lost* itself, the decree was not old and was self-imposed – the vow that all four young men made to spend two years in the academy, abiding by the rigid restrictions they had invented for themselves. In *A Midsummer Night's Dream* it took the form of Duke Theseus's support of Egeus's demand that Hermia should marry Demetrius. Here, in *The Merchant of Venice*, it is twofold. Firstly, there is Portia's father's stipulation in the will that his daughter must marry the man who passes the test of the three caskets. Secondly, there is Shylock's bond. But these are not really variants of the same thing. The will is in fact not a restriction at all, since it acts as a brake on the attentions of undesirable suitors and actually permits Portia to marry Bassanio, the man she wants. The bond, on the other hand, is an undesirable impediment to the happiness of that marriage, and must be destroyed before a happy conclusion is possible.

There is one significant difference between Shylock's role as a potentially tragic impediment to the comic conclusion, and that of all the other examples – not just the lovers' vows and Egeus's threats, but also Oliver's hatred of Orlando in *As You Like It* and Duke Frederick's hatred of Rosalind in the same play. Shylock constitutes a persistent, visible, and dramatic threat throughout the play. He appears three times as such between the scene in which the original bargain was made (I, iii) and the courtroom scene in which it is rendered impotent (IV, i) – four times if we include the first half of the courtroom scene itself, before Portia enters. Other scenes suggest the danger – those, for example, in which Lorenzo contrives his elopement with Jessica, and also those in which the subliminal imagery is strongly present. These last remind us of the precariousness of Antonio's fortunes, and so of his life, which is forfeit to the Jew. Take this speech by Gratiano at II, vi, which is spoken in a scene otherwise unconcerned with Antonio. Salerio has reminded Gratiano of the way the need to possess the beloved far exceeds the need to be faithful to her when she is possessed. Gratiano replies that:

All things that are
Are with more spirit chased than enjoy'd.
How like a younker or a prodigal
The scarfed bark puts from her native bay,
Hugg'd and embraced by the strumpet wind.
How like the prodigal doth she return,
With over-weather'd ribs and ragged sails,
Lean, rent and beggar'd by the strumpet wind!

The sense has nothing whatever to do with Antonio's ships. Even so the imagery cannot help but call them to mind. What if they also return with overweathered ribs and ragged sails, or not at all? We are forcefully reminded of the danger in which he will be placed if the fortune fails to materialise and the bond is claimed.

In other words, the narrative line is strong, and plot is much more important than it was in *Love's Labour's Lost* or even *A Midsummer Night's Dream*. The last act is again reserved for minor business (the rings) and lyrical effusion (Lorenzo and Jessica) but what has preceded it relies much more on events than had been the case in either of the two earlier comedies. It is, in Barber's words, much less of a theatrical adaptation of a social ritual than they were. This is because of Shylock. He exists as a visible complication to the smooth running of Bassanio's friendship with Antonio and his courtship of Portia. In other words he is the character who makes the plot possible. But this plot is so insisted upon, it is made to seem so real, that a kind of suspense is produced that no one in *Love's Labour's Lost* or *A Midsummer Night's Dream* ever seriously felt. There is a grim irony in Shylock's mention of 'a merry sport', 'this merry bond' in the first Act. The sense of play is much less strong here than it has been before.

Shylock does this. Does he do more? Does he also have a key position in the expression of the themes of the play? These can be defined as the display of contrary modes of conduct viewed in the light of two main activities: economic and legal. The first takes the form of a study of the means of getting and using wealth – by trade or by finance, i.e. usury. The second takes the form of a study of the relation between positive and natural law

– what the law can do and what it should do. The legal aspect takes up almost the whole of Act IV, and is mainly confined to that act. In it, I see no way of getting round the fact that the dice are transparently loaded against Shylock – and neither does anyone else. But the economic aspect is different. It has become fashionable to build up a case against the Venetians on the grounds that they are guilty, albeit in an attractive and 'rhetorical' way, of an 'unseemly covetousness' which is no better than the a-social miserliness represented by Shylock. Thus Shylock's villainy is somewhat mitigated and brought within the scope of a humanist debate. His is just one form of unbecoming conduct, in respect of the uses of money, among others that are widespread among Christians in Venice. It is therefore used to show up the corruption of the Venetians as much as to draw attention to that of itself.

This leads one recent editor of *The Merchant of Venice* (W. Moelwyn Merchant) to conclude that 'ironic judgement is suspended as deftly over the decadent acquisitiveness of the Venetians as it is brought to bear on the greed of Shylock and Tubal'. Shakespeare rarely takes sides, we are told; the appropriate words to apply to the play are 'moral judgment', 'poise', 'detachment'. The imagery is suggestive in a much more subtle sense than I have shown. When Jessica includes Medea in her list of lovers (at the opening of v, i), sinister implications attach to the name. A comparison is drawn between Portia and Medea, and a corresponding treachery and greed insinuated into the relation between Portia and Bassanio, and all they stand for. After all, Medea is associated with the golden fleece, which has been referred to more than once in the play; and in the end Jason deserted her for Glauce, the daughter of the King of Corinth. This is all very well, but is there really much of a hint that Bassanio's love for Portia is like that of Jason for Medea, with similar aims and very likely the same consequences? Even here, there is nothing very sinister about Medea gathering herbs. In the legend she did so with no evil intent, simply to renew the youth and vigour of Jason's father Aeson – though it is true that in some versions of the story he had to be boiled in a cauldron to make it possible. Once one starts this kind of search for ironic comparisons and contrasts, all poems and plays are converted into *Waste Lands*, without notes. Surely the terms according to which *The*

Merchant of Venice conducts itself preclude this sort of super-sophistication?

What is happening is that a critique of the Venetian courtier–traders is being manufactured, where no such critique exists in the play we have. If it is there, then Shylock can be integrated into the *Merchant* as a contributor to a debate on the use of riches which is conducted on a level at which the phrases Moelwyn Merchant uses are wholly appropriate. Shylock is no longer an eruptive force that damages the desirable comic–romance fabric of the play as a whole. Instead he is a carefully controlled device for modulating our responses to the Venetians, for manoeuvring us into a position from which we are enabled to judge them as harshly as we judge him. Both are complementary aberrations from a correct behavioural norm.

Such a view seems to me to be misconceived and to be based upon a false idea of the nature of Shakespeare's stagecraft and of the kinds of theatrical effect he could command by the mid-1590s. It assumes two things which I do not think it is permissible to assume: one, that *The Merchant of Venice* is an entirely successful play; and two, that it is a particular kind of successful play, one in which poised ironic judgements are a part of 'a process of nice critical casuistry'. Shakespeare turns out to be an Augustan before his time, thinking in terms of balanced opinions and antithetical points of view that many scholars like to think are synonymous with maturity, the quality above all others that great writers are supposed to possess. I think Shakespeare's maturity, his wisdom, is of a very different nature. The poise and judgement that had some relevance to *Love's Labour's Lost* and even to parts of *A Midsummer Night's Dream* are not so much to the forefront. The ironic wit with which Shakespeare handled the illusions and false notions of reality the lovers possessed there is replaced here with a romantic, lyrical endorsement of the lovers' values – which breaks down under the pressure of Shylock's eruption into the play-world. Antonio, Bassanio, Lorenzo and Gratiano are not made to look foolish, as the King's men and Demetrius and Lysander were in the earlier plays. Their romantic attachments are underwritten from the beginning.

An interpretation of the play which focuses on contrasts between equally reprehensible groups and individuals is therefore out of place. The contrast is not a fine one between values which are part good and part bad. It is a bold one between the villain Shylock and the hero Antonio – and Bassanio, Gratiano and the others. Equally, there is little thematic contrast between the worlds of Venice and Belmont. The only contrast is one between a place where money is made – in the most romantic manner possible; and a place where what it is spent on is made sumptuously visible. The one is characterised by light and sunshine, the other by moonlight and music. Both of them manage to absorb the language of currency, finance and trade into a world of romantic love and elevated friendship. In both cases Shylock's attitude to money is contrasted with that of the Christians. He sees it as so much gold that can be put to work to produce more gold. They see it as an opportunity to increase the pleasures of friendship and society. This is as true of Belmont as of Venice, with the exception that we see even less of how it is got hold of in Portia's house than we did on the Rialto.

The language the Venetians speak is not so much witty as, again, romantic. It is more swelling, plastic, malleable and fulsome than ever before, except in one or two speeches from *A Midsummer Night's Dream* and those of the lovers in *Romeo and Juliet*. A good example of it is this, at the very opening of the play, where Salerio and Solanio are trying to explain to Antonio why he is so sad and has 'so much ado to know himself':

> Your mind [says Salerio] is tossing on the ocean;
> There where your argosies, with portly sail –
> Like signiors and rich burghers on the flood,
> Or as it were the pageants of the sea –
> Do overpeer the petty traffickers,
> That curtsy to them, do them reverence,
> As they fly by them with their woven wings.

If he went to church and caught a glimpse of the stone it was built of, and if at the same time he were in Antonio's position, Salerio would bethink him straight of dangerous rocks

> Which, touching but my gentle vessel's side,
> Would scatter all her spices on the stream,

Enrobe the roaring waters with my silks,
And, in a word, but even now worth this,
And now worth nothing.

This, and much more. Each line moves in stately procession to its
close and pauses there to gather up the rich trail of imagery it has
laid. There is little of the flickering dance across the line endings
that Shakespeare had already made use of in *A Midsummer
Night's Dream*. The movement is more impressive than ever
before, but it is not rapid. The imagery combines a vivid impression of an actual scene with an imaginative response to the
scene on the part of the speaker; and the result is that the words
extend outwards to connect with other words spoken by other
speakers which, taken together, build up a very dense picture of
the Venetian setting – more in terms of atmosphere than topo-
graphy. Gratiano and Nerissa give a witty edge to the setting
they belong to, preventing the impression from being over-ripe.
The language points the same way as the plot. Shakespeare does
not want to 'show up' the questionable values of the Venice–
Belmont world (or worlds, if you feel the distinction must be
insisted upon). Instead he intends to use those values – of generosity, courtesy, gaiety and love – to resist the malevolent force of
Shylock and his bond.

That certainly seems to have been Shakespeare's intention.
Nonetheless, these values are shown up. They are shown up as
comic–romance values which are unable to resist the 'reality' of
Shylock's complex humanity. Part of the trouble is that the plot
that Shakespeare took over for his casket story (another romance,
this time from Richard Robinson's translation of the *Gesta
Romanorum* in 1577) has brought out deep-seated contradictions
in his treatment of young fortune-hunters. There are plenty of
examples of these characters elsewhere in the comedies. We have
already noticed Proteus's caddish behaviour towards Julia in *The
Two Gentlemen of Verona*. There are also Claudio's treatment
of Hero in *Much Ado about Nothing*, Bertram's of Helena in
All's Well that Ends Well, and, with saving graces in mid-play,
Posthumus's of Imogen in *Cymbeline*. There is something
unsatisfactory about all these young men, who are strangely compounded in equal parts of the most noble idealism and the most
intolerable expediency, usually in money matters. Bassanio shares

something of their two-faced character, which is neither hypocrisy nor life-like ambivalence, and it makes him a difficult character to come to terms with.

All the more difficult in that he carries a double handicap. The callow young man has to woo a passive young woman. Usually Shakespeare's heroines are very spirited – alert, intelligent, always ready to take the initiative. Portia does this herself from Act IV onwards. But before this time she is prevented from showing any active spirit by the three caskets that stand between her and the real life of choices that would prove her mettle. As Portia retires behind the caskets, Bassanio advances towards them. The only active thing he does in the whole play, except borrow money from Antonio, is to choose the right casket. Naturally, therefore, we attach a great deal of importance to the way he does this; and the way he does it is odd, to say the least.

Why does Bassanio choose the lead casket? The only reason I can think of is so that he can be allowed to marry Portia. There is nothing in his character to suggest that he is likely to do anything but choose 'by the view'. Antonio, not Bassanio, is the person in the play who gives and hazards all he has. Bassanio's character is decidedly 'golden' – 'who chooseth me shall gain what many men desire.' We *know* that he is interested in the golden side of Portia because the first thing he says about her is that she is a lady 'richly left'. Only after that does he explain that she is 'fair' and 'Of wondrous virtues'.

Others have felt something of the incongruity of his correct but thoroughly inappropriate choice. Some have tried to get round the problem by making Portia more positive than she has been allowed to be. They point out that in the song that is sung as Bassanio makes his decision, the first three end words conspicuously rhyme with 'lead'. Well, so do the last three of the jingle the Prince of Arragon finds in the casket, and none of the same critics has suggested that Portia's father had unwittingly hit on the same idea and converted it into a sick joke. Besides, it is inconsistent with what character Portia has that she should descend to a cheap trick. And imagine ruining a lovely song by tying it to a knowing grimace and a mangled tune.

Others have got round the problem by pointing out that Bassanio's conduct is consistent with the underlying theme of the play which is not, as I have described it and as it appears to be on the surface, a critique of certain views about wealth and law, but an assessment of the different ways in which feeling and judgement affect the actions of various individuals. According to those who hold this view, the words of the song are important not because of what they sound like but because of what they say. 'Fancy' is Bassanio's love for Portia. Is it going to succeed by moral deliberation ('the head' – his peroration on 'outward shows' before making his choice) or by an emotional attunement to the appropriate mood ('the heart' – succumbing to the power of the music, which induces the solemn mood required to provoke the choice of the least glittering casket)? The same theme is supposed to surface again in the trial scene, where Portia's reasoned speech about mercy fails to dissuade Shylock from demanding his pound of flesh, but where her casuistical argument about taking not a jot of blood succeeds. This seems to me to be no more satisfactory than the rhyme explanation, because I see no reason to suppose that the song would of itself induce not merely a solemn mood, but a solemn mood which is appropriate to the choice of a lead, rather than a gold or a silver casket (Is solemnity somehow unprecious, a leaden virtue?). Also it seems to me that in the trial scene Portia's speech about mercy is not notable for its logical, as distinct from its rhetorical and forensic, power; and that the argument about the jot of blood, whilst certainly casuistical, is logically respectable. Casuistical arguments usually are. They impose on one's powers of judgement, not one's capacity for feeling.

We are in a cleft stick. If the caskets represent a fair test of character Bassanio, to be virtuous as well as to ensure that *The Merchant of Venice* remains a comedy, must choose the right one – which he does. On the other hand, to choose the right one he must have the appropriate character – which he does not. It follows that either he wins Portia by a trick, which is unthinkable; or Shakespeare unrealistically manipulates his character to suit the occasion, which is much more likely. In itself, this is not a cardinal sin in a romantic comedy. What makes it awkward here is that the realism with which Shylock's character is presented encourages us to question the springs of behaviour in a way we would not have dreamed of doing in the earlier plays. We are disposed to apply criteria for the interpretation of character which are appropriate to the case of Shylock, to others who simply cannot stand up to them. In the face of Shylock's eruption into the play, the comic procedures that govern the conduct of the Venetians prove to be totally inadequate, and the psychological anomalies of what is intended for the main plot stand out in a harsh light whenever we are reminded of the Jew. As I have pointed out, we are reminded of him a lot of the time, since the part he plays in events is so much greater than that of his pallid forebears, who knew their place and didn't get in the way.

But we get it all wrong if we suppose that the anomalies and contradictions which spring from this were intended to be there. They are not a part of Shakespeare's critique of the values of courtly trade – decadent acquisitiveness, an emergent capitalist society. They are the unlooked-for consequences of the combination of an unsuitable source and a maldistribution of the main characters. Bassanio's central position in the plot had to bring out the worst in him or make him contradict himself. Shylock's emergence as a fascinatingly complex non-romance character ensures that when Bassanio *does* contradict himself we notice it, and notice also how flimsy a character he is. Neither he nor Portia can be expected to succeed in shoring up the artifice of the romance plotting against the real and damaging psychological substance of Shylock.

As for Shylock himself, he is no fit subject for a book on Shakespeare's comic art. In the end, Dogget was miscast for the part. Oddly enough, though, Shakespeare did not take him up and develop him in a tragic setting. It is typical of his genius that he did that with a very much slighter part. Six years later the Prince of Morocco stepped out of romance into reality in the figure of Othello. Shylock remains a splendid gargoyle stuck to the edifice of a fairy palace, a testament to Shakespeare's careless habit of conspicuous waste.

6

Falstaff

The only one of Shakespeare's plays that has Falstaff as its central character is *The Merry Wives of Windsor*, and it is generally agreed that the Falstaff in it is a very pale reflection of the Falstaff we feel we know. When we think of Falstaff, we think of him as he appears in the two parts of *Henry IV*, the fat knight whose banter with Hal, Poins, Mistress Quickly and the Lord Chief Justice provides the comic sub-plot of these plays. Removed from the Boar's Head tavern and his Eastcheap friends and flung into the parlours of the Elizabethan bourgeoisie, his bulk remained but his spirit dwindled. So, in writing about Falstaff, I shall be writing about the man who appears in the two history plays, and not the impostor in the buck-basket.

It makes a lot of difference that I am discussing a character and not a play. The comedies do not reveal their secrets in the personality of any one of the characters. By their forms shall you know them, by which I mean the arrangements within which all the characters define their several ideas and attributes. *As You Like It* is not about Rosalind in the same way as *Hamlet* is about the Prince of Denmark. But I have to make an exception of Falstaff. Of course, *Henry IV Parts 1* and *2* are not about him. They are about the capacity of private persons to enact public roles, the relationship between private conscience and political action. But, as we consider the position Falstaff ocupies in the dramatic exposition of this subject, we are bound to see how he grows out of it, how he not so much overwhelms the plays as acquires a presence and a personality somehow apart from them. One foot remains in historical narrative, the other clumps about outside of it, giving the impression that his great bulk is at the same time firmly set in a precise context of actions and relationships, and floating above them in a world where place, time, and plot are of no consequence. What Falstaff *does* and what he *is* often seem to have little or nothing to do with each other.

Let us look first at his position in the narrative. I have said that it is a narrative given over to the exposition of a theme: that of the relationship between private and public identity. The nature of the public activity changes from *Part 1* to *Part 2*. In *Part 1* it is mainly military, and the theme of the play is that of chivalry, or honour. In *Part 2* it is mainly political, and the theme is that of government, or authority. I propose to have a closer look at *Part 1* to bring out the role Falstaff plays in the dramatisation of the theme, in this case of the idea of chivalry, which means that for the space of five minutes or so we shall have to leave the comic business to deal with weightier matters. But we shall understand the comedy better when we return to it.

The two most important political characters in *1 Henry IV* are Prince Hal and Hotspur, and their fundamentally different approaches to life are set off, or highlighted, by the attitudes they adopt towards the governing idea of honour. Contrary to what most people suppose, Falstaff has very little to *say* about honour. Outside of his big speech on the subject at v, ii, ('What is honour?' etc.) he rarely talks about it. He prefers to demonstrate his attitude towards honour – which is at every opportunity to subordinate it to self-preservation – by *doing* things: running away from the robbers and then justifying himself in thoroughly unspeculative terms back at the Boar's Head. In this respect he is very different from Hal and Hotspur. Hotspur has most to say about honour. His speech about plucking up drowned honour by the locks is just about the most famous serious one in the play. Hal, on the other hand, values honour for public rather than for private reasons. He talks about it in financial terms as a 'factor' to be 'redeemed' at the best possible moment. What is for Hotspur something infinitely romantic and therefore desirable in itself, an end in itself, is for Hal just one among many things that it is necessary a ruler should possess, a means not an end, in a world where means are as important as ends, and difficult to distinguish from them. So Hal is conscious of honour, but does not feel constrained to speak about it all the time because it is not a quality that compels, but is itself the object of compulsions of a very different and more public nature.

Hotspur's attitude towards honour shows him to be adolescent, romantic, simultaneously self-concerned and self-ignorant, impulsive, imaginative and potentially tragic. Hal's shows him to be adult, pragmatic, unself-concerned but fully aware of his limitations, prudent, pedestrian in his all-round accomplishments, not the stuff that tragedy is made of. Not everyone will agree with this brief summing-up. But I think they will agree that the characters of both men are compounded of qualities both good and not so good. At some points they are sympathetic, at others not. What I think Falstaff does is make us think again, by his very presence, about qualities in each of the other two characters which we might otherwise have found utterly unsympathetic. In many respects, Hal seems a cold fish; admirable perhaps, but hardly lovable. Yet Falstaff loves him. 'I am bewitched with the rogue's company' he says. 'If the rascal have not given me medicines to make me love him, I'll be hanged.' Hotspur is often infuriating in his childish greed for self-esteem. But, when at Shrewsbury Falstaff pierces his dead body with a sword, we are forced to look again at Hotspur's values, which would never have allowed him to do such a despicable thing. There may be more to a person and to the values he embodies than we are normally prepared to admit. Falstaff is in the play to make sure we do not make too predictable judgements on the behaviour of either of the protagonists. He is the character who all the time is saying – 'There may be more to this than meets the eye.'

He does the same thing in a different way immediately before the stabbing incident in Act v. The play contrives to interest us in a character's ability to be, as well as to develop and contribute to the expression of an idea. Hal is not very good at 'being'. When he steps forward as a private person, as in his soliloquy ('I know you all . . .') at the end of I, ii, he fails to commit himself to privacy. His words are all concerned with publicity – 'imitate', 'please you to be himself', 'playing', throwing off loose behaviour and making offence a skill. Hal never fails to calculate, and when we watch him in the Eastcheap scenes we find ourselves doing two things: complimenting him on the ease with which he disguises his real intentions behind a mask of wit and humour; and enjoying the wit and humour for their own sake, as if Hal were not Hal. Hotspur has a greater ability to exist for himself. His love of honour doesn't entirely prevent him from coming across as a warm human being – in his relations with his wife, or with Glendower for example. His character is unfixed – what appear to be the roles he plays are not really roles at all, but real parts of a whole, but unformed, personality. Hal has become what he is and all he is ever going to be – except for the external trappings of throne and crown. He can therefore pretend to be what he is not, and entertain us by the way he uses that pretence. But Hotspur is a character still in the process of being formed. Perhaps he will never grow up. Because he is a character at war with himself, because of contradictions in his character which he does not understand, he is to my mind a more interesting person than Hal.

We can now return to Act v. Hotspur, mortally wounded, makes the most philosophical and meditative speech in the play. But he is cut off in mid-sentence, and the speech has to be completed by Hal, who fails to rise to the occasion. The witty lines on the size of a dead man's grave, anticipating Hamlet on Alexander, are better than the references to favours, rites and epitaphs that follow. These make it clear that Hal is still playing the game (of chivalry) that Hotspur has shown to be irrelevant in his death speech. Then Hal notices Falstaff's apparently dead body close by, and his couplet speech tries to place him in the 'honour' context along with Hotspur. But both of them, Hotspur in death and Falstaff in life, have passed beyond it. The comic juxtaposition of the two men, and the separation of Hal from both, gives a picture of the distance Hotspur has come and the lack of awareness Hal has shown all along of the fact that there might be a distance to go. It is Falstaff, lying between the two of them, who makes the point most vividly.

I don't expect everybody to agree with me that this is precisely how Falstaff functions in the play, but I think many would see the part he plays in those sort of terms. My point is that though they are relevant, they are incomplete. They only deal with the foot that is stuck in the historical narrative. It seems to me that the modern approach to the play has often sought to belittle Falstaff, to cut him down to size by insisting overmuch on his role in the history. Throughout, he is known to be an enlargement of a character in the source (*The Famous Victories of Henry V*) who was called Sir John Oldcastle, a name changed to Falstaff in deference, probably, to the Cobham family, who had important positions at Court and were therefore not to be alienated by an ambitious playwright. Then in *Part 1* he is clearly an adaptation of the Plautan *Miles Gloriosus* and in *Part 2* of the Morality Vice with prototypes in fifteenth-century plays like *Lusty Juventus*,

The Castle of Perseverance, and *Nature*. In *Part 1* he is actually called a Vice, Iniquity, Vanity by Hal when he is acting the king. Altogether there is plenty of opportunity for those who like to reduce characters to the sum of their background originals.

This was especially likely to happen to Falstaff because from the late seventeenth century to the nineteenth century critics had often reduced the plays to plays about Falstaff. The most recent example of this is Orson Welles's film *Chimes at Midnight*, in which Falstaff appears at the centre of a piece which also includes, as subsidiary characters, such figures as Hal, the King, the rebels and so on. But more often there has been a reaction against such handling of the *Henry IV* plays. Either they are treated like nineteenth-century novels, with Hal as a picaresque hero and Falstaff as a Micawber-like 'grotesque'. Or they are viewed as dramatised Elizabethan world pictures with the emphasis firmly on the ritual and history, with Hal in the most important position as the prince who must prepare himself for his proper place in the political hierarchy. Falstaff then plays the supporting role of tempter to the prince, again in a fleshed-out Morality fashion. The only alternative has been to make of Falstaff a main character cast in a nineteenth-century mould. The questions to ask about him remain the same as those Maurice Morgann asked as early as 1777, in his *Dramatic Character of Sir John Falstaff*: is he a coward or isn't he? Why did he fall asleep behind the arras? Did he really recognise Hal at Gadshill or didn't he? Again this is beside the point, or it is only a small part of the point. Let us look at Falstaff from another angle altogether.

From the beginning, Falstaff has been approached differently from any other of Shakespeare's characters. For Dryden 'the very sight of such an unwieldy old debauched fellow is a comedy alone' and Dr Johnson found him unimitated and inimitable. The only comparable figure in the plays is Hamlet. But there is one large difference. Hamlet has usually been admired because he possesses what his admirer supposes are the best, or at any rate the most interesting qualities in himself. Coleridge is not the only poet or critic who has indulged in a game of romantic self-identification with the melancholy hero. Nobody, so far as I know, has taken upon himself the character of Falstaff. Johnson admired him because of his most pleasing of all qualities, 'perpetual gaiety . . . an unfailing power of exciting laughter'. Falstaff is always different from the person who writes about him. He is viewed in a perspective of affection and of love. Because he doesn't threaten us, or flatter us, we do not feel the need to make him over into a version of ourselves. We are prepared to take him as he is, because he takes us as we are.

'I am not only witty in myself,' he says to his page at the beginning of *Part 2* 'but the cause that wit is in other men.' That is the secret of his popularity. By the play of his own wit he gives us a renewed sense of our own. The laws of the workaday world in which we live are for the most part suspended, and we enter into another world, with laws of a completely different kind. Here the judgements we are customarily forced to make on people and events (because of our sense of responsibility, our feeling that the world's work must be done) become liberatingly irrelevant. This is why accusations of cowardice (at Gadshill) and cruelty (to the recruits) are out of place. When we enter Falstaff's world we switch over to a different order of priorities – and morality, the consideration that makes us take such a serious view of robbing pilgrims and enlisting men for the army according to the amount of money they can or cannot pay, is not high on the list. Falstaff's world is liberating because it is amoral. We appreciate people according to their liveliness or vitality; and because Falstaff makes *us* feel more alive, more witty, we pay him the compliment of abandoning judgement on him on any but his own terms. I am going to qualify this in a moment. It is where we start from, not where we end. Shakespeare does play tricks from time to time by having Falstaff walk into the workaday world of warfare and politics – at Shrewsbury for example. But on the whole, certainly in *Part 1*, we are inside Falstaff's world when he is on the stage and so we abide by its rules, not the rules that apply to the public action outside of it. Looking at the world of Henry, Northumberland and Worcester, the world Hal really belongs to, we can see that Falstaff's world is not better than this world, but that the two are incompatible. The laws that apply to the one cannot apply to the other.

That is what Falstaff's behaviour at the Boar's Head, before the sheriff and his watch arrive, has to tell us. It has little to do with whether Falstaff is a coward or a stoic. The most important word in th: scene, the word that tells us more about Falstaff than any other is 'instinct'. 'Beware instinct', says Falstaff. 'Instinct is a great matter. I was now a coward on instinct.' Most productions emphasise the wrong word. When the assembled company have heard the news of the impending battle, Falstaff asks Hal 'Doth thy blood thrill at it?' Hal remains unimpressed. 'Not a wit, i' faith,' he replies, 'I lack some of thy instinct.' Certainly he does. His whole life is dedicated to the cultivation of an inner consistency of purpose that holds firm beneath the mercurial changes of expression and personality he displays to both his stage and theatre audiences. Falstaff, on the contrary, has no feeling for or understanding of consistency. His instinct is a sense of the moment and a capacity for inspired improvisation. We can never get to the bottom of Falstaff's chopping and changing. Where Hal's disguises are skin deep, Falstaff's have no bottom. Take away his lies and his performances and he does not exist.

The contrast, not merely between personalities, but between theatrical creations too, is clearest in respect of the characters' attitudes to time. Never before has time played such an important part in a play by Shakespeare as it does here, especially in *Part 2*. The 'politicians' are obsessed by it for, after all, time is the essence of their plans. Hal will redeem time when men least think he will; Worcester wishes the state of time had first been whole before Northumberland had fallen sick; Hotspur dies in the belief that life is time's fool; Hastings says that the rebels are time's subjects, and time bids them be gone; and the Archbishop thinks he has seen the way the stream of time doth run, which explains his presence on the battlefield at Gaultree forest. They are aware of the passage of time; aware also of their subjection to it. Their business is therefore to accommodate themselves to it to their greatest advantage. There is a poem by W. H. Auden called 'Our Bias' which gives an optimistic twist to the same idea. The characters here, however, are not optimistic. Accommodation is a dire necessity, not an amusing game. The only people who are amused are those who can forget time altogether, and they are few. Fortunately for us they include Falstaff.

The first words Hal speaks to Falstaff are about time. 'What the devil hast thou to do with the time of day?' he replies to Falstaff's own question about the time. Falstaff couldn't have been serious. He has nothing to do with time. In both plays he fails to synchronise with it. In the middle of the battle at Shrewsbury Hal finds a bottle of sack in Falstaff's pistol case. 'What!' he asks 'is it a time to jest and dally now?' Falstaff is unabashed. What difference does the time make to jesting and dallying? In *Part 2* the Lord Chief Justice is scandalised by Falstaff's quarrel with Mistress Quickly. 'Doth this become your place, your time, and business?' he asks. But what is all this about time? 'My lord,' says Falstaff, 'I was born about three of the clock in the afternoon, with a white head and something of a round belly . . . to approve my youth further I will not. The truth is, I am only old in judgment and understanding.' In fact there is plenty of evidence that Falstaff is showing his age. The description the Lord Chief Justice gives of him is hardly that of the irresistible *grand seigneur* he likes to think he is, and the doctor takes a poor view of his water. Nevertheless, Falstaff represents an apparent triumph over time. Unlike the political characters, he ignores time, and refuses to entertain the belief that time will not ignore him. Some of the gloom that people notice in this play when they compare it with its predecessor comes from the more and more pressing evidence that he is wrong.

Back in *Richard II* it was the serious characters who came to acknowledge this. In the dungeon of Pomfret Castle, Richard himself had begun to realise that 'I wasted time, and now doth time waste me.' The same thing begins to dawn on Falstaff in *Henry IV Part 2*. In *Part 1* his energetic illusionism worked. Time really did stand still when he was on the stage. We forgot all about it too. What the devil did we have to do with the time of day? In *Part 2* it falters, and then fails. The sense of physical decay is overwhelming, and Falstaff himself cannot avoid remembering his end. What has happened, then, since *Part 1*? Has Falstaff suddenly grown older?

Falstaff doesn't age between the two plays. He was old in *Part 1*, but Shakespeare prevented us from noticing it. He did this by a very simple device. In *Part 1* Falstaff always had a stage audience and a foil to play to. The stage audience comprised the company at the Boar's Head; the foil was Hal. This enabled him to improvise artificial situations in which we, the outer audience, became involved. Now if we are involved in something, thoroughly engrossed, we lose all sense of time and age. In *Part 1* this was happening all the time, pre-eminently in II, iv, with the double play of Falstaff and Hal as king and heir. In *Part 2* the stage audience is still there. But the foil that brought it to life before is gone. Hal is with the court. He approaches the Boar's Head from the outside, and we come in from the outside too. So Falstaff is left in the company of the old. True, he has a boy to carry his sword and buckler and make the appropriate noises. But the boy is not Hal. He does not bounce back and provide Falstaff with the challenge to be funny. Even the jokes about Bardolph's nose become strained and repetitive. Bardolph himself, and Peto, have not much of a part between them. The Falstaff plot has to be filled out with relics like the Lord Chief Justice, Mistress Quickly, Shallow and Silence, and there's not much opportunity given by any of them for the raucous good humour that drove away the time in the earlier play.

The lack of the sense of play we had grown used to makes us take up a more detached attitude to what is going on. Take the Gloucestershire scenes, and Falstaff's speech on Shallow at the end of III, ii:

I do see the bottom of Justice Shallow. Lord, Lord, how subject we old men are to this vice of lying! This same starv'd justice hath done nothing but prate to me of the wildness of his youth and the feats he hath done about Turnbull Street; and every third word a lie, duer paid to the hearer than the Turk's tribute. I do remember him at Clement's Inn, like a man made after supper of a cheese-paring. When 'a was naked, he was for all the world like a fork'd radish, with a head fantastically carved upon it with a knife. 'A was so forlorn that his dimensions to any thick sight were invisible. 'A was the very genius of famine; yet lecherous as a monkey, and the whores call'd him mandrake. 'A came ever in the rearward of the fashion, and sung those tunes to the over-scutch'd huswifes that he heard the carmen whistle, and sware they were his fancies or his good-nights. And now is this Vice's dagger become a squire, and talks as familiarly of John a Gaunt as if he had been sworn brother to him; and I'll be sworn 'a ne'er saw him but once in the Tiltyard; and then he burst his head for crowding among the marshal's men. I saw it, and told John a Gaunt he beat his own name; for you might have thrust him and all his apparel into an eel-skin; the case of a treble hautboy was a mansion for him, a court – and now has he land and beeves. Well, I'll be acquainted with him if I return; and't shall go hard but I'll make him a philosopher's two stones to me. If the young dace be a bait for the old pike, I see no reason in the law of nature but I may snap at him. Let time shape, and there an end.

It begins as a shrewd commentary on the deceptions of age and ends as a capitulation to those same deceptions. The fact that Falstaff includes himself in the habit of mind he is criticising makes no difference. We notice the self-deception of the speech from the outside, we cannot involve ourselves in it. And though we are tolerant, we are also sad. His last words still disclaim any involvement with time, but they are resigned, defeated, more like Hastings in i, iii than like himself in ii, iv of *Part 1*.

In *Henry IV Part 2* we are seeing Falstaff as he was in *Part 1* but from the outside. We have been pulled away from the charmed circle of the illusion he had created there, and we see him with a detached eye through which we had seldom looked before. Unmixed humour and delight have given way to a sense of pathos and alienation, which is reinforced by everything we see in the play, outside the Falstaff scenes as well as in them. Not just politics, and Hal's world in which they belong, have caught up with him in the end, but time, age, mortality – the real world which he had previously been able to play with and control. The recruits who had only been spoken about in *Part 1* appear in *Part 2*. They have names, they have characters, and they have families. Falstaff's treatment of them is no longer funny. He is defeated as much by the real world as he is by Hal. Indeed, Hal is no more than the dramatic means whereby reality takes its revenge on him.

There is an ironic parallel between Hal and Falstaff in the last scene. Both of them appear in their proper roles – that of the king and that of the fool. Hal knows that it is all a great dramatic spectacle. But he has no need to fear. His youth, position and hereditary right protect him, make him invulnerable from the outside. Falstaff had never consciously pretended to be what he was not. His whole life was based on a different principle. So he is surprised when events begin to overtake him. He has to suppose the King will repent. Otherwise the illusions which sustained him throughout the plays will fall away, and he will be exposed as the 'extra' he is, the man in the crowd, the dispensable clown whose wrinkles show through the greasepaint.

I know thee not, old man. Fall to thy prayers.
How ill white hairs become a fool and jester.

That is what we began to realise from the beginning of *Part 2*. Falstaff had kept it at bay until now. The King moves past the man he has destroyed without batting an eyelid. It is no use speculating on whether sending him to the Fleet was a kindness or a punishment. I doubt Falstaff ever got there.

7

Much Ado about Nothing and All's Well that Ends Well

These two plays are often considered the least satisfactory of Shakespeare's mature comedies, and I must say I share the prevailing dissatisfaction. My reasons for this are not altogether the same in each case, but they are not altogether *not* the same either. Let me explain.

Much Ado about Nothing and *All's Well that Ends Well* are separated from each other by at least four years. *Much Ado* was written in either 1598 or 1599. *All's Well* is more difficult to date because it is not mentioned in any of the contemporary records, there is no Quarto version (i.e. separate publication, before the Folio edition of *all* the plays in 1623), the first recorded performance was as late as 1741, and the style it is written in is eclectic. It is assumed that it was written at some time between 1602 and 1604. The later play therefore falls into the period of Shakespeare's so called problem comedies, about which I shall have more to say in my chapter on *Measure for Measure*. *Much Ado*, on the other hand, precedes the two great 'romantic' comedies, *As You Like It* and *Twelfth Night*. However, I think both of these plays are problems, and I want to elaborate on the different ways they go about being problems. That is why I have interrupted the chronological sequence I observe elsewhere, and chosen to deal with *All's Well* in advance of its proper time.

To begin with the problem they have in common, I mean the hero. It seems to me that much of the difficulty of both these plays is created by the behaviour of the heroes, or, to be more precise, the young men whose central position in the plot would lead us to believe that is what they are intended to be. Claudio and Bertram are much of a likeness. Claudio may be a little older, having seen active service in the battles referred to in the first scene of *Much Ado*. But these appear to have comprised his first military engagement, since a good deal is made of his youth and the promise of his age, which he is said to have borne himself beyond. He has performed the feats of a lion 'in the figure of a lamb'. Bertram we know is young enough to be made a ward of court to the King of France. In a play that places heavy emphasis on the contrast between youth and age, he is singled out as conspicuously youthful and inexperienced in the ways of the world.

Youth is a property they share along with many other less superficial similarities. Few of these redound to their credit. Briefly, they are smug, selfish, callow, ill-tempered, unimaginative, outwardly polished and inwardly tarnished. 'Scambling, out-facing, fashion-monging boys', Antonio says in *Much Ado*. I think their behaviour warrants this sort of unequivocal moral judgement. Each of them is a fully developed specimen of the type sketched out in Proteus, the hero of Shakespeare's first experiment in romantic comedy, *The Two Gentlemen of Verona*. We encountered the type again in Bassanio, whose unsatisfactory character did much to upset our response to the main plot of *The Merchant of Venice*. But I made the point that we would not have got so upset about Bassanio if Shylock had not been there to encourage us to expect more (in the way of character and psychological appropriateness) than the hero was able to offer. In these two later plays the heroes behave much more culpably than Bassanio did over the wooing of Portia. In any case, what we are concerned about is the way they run away from the girl, not how they pursue her, and that makes a considerable difference. So the presence of the Shylock figure is not necessary. Don John is a poor substitute in *Much Ado*. There is no villain in *All's Well*. The heroes contrive to place themselves in a critical perspective without any external help.

Nevertheless, the way the rest of the play organises itself around their characters does produce interesting differences in our responses to them. Whilst Claudio's caddish renunciation of Hero strikes an audience as a dramatic mistake (a mistake which the author may have foreseen and which seems to have coloured his treatment of the Claudio–Hero scenes from the start), Bertram's at least equally caddish renunciation of Helena, repeated with nauseating regularity throughout *All's Well*, seems entirely appropriate to the play to which he belongs. *Much Ado* doesn't represent itself as the sort of play in which Claudio's 'rotten orange' speech is at all appropriate. *All's Well* does represent itself as the sort of play in which Bertram's 'Disdain/Rather corrupt me ever' fits very well indeed. I am implying that Shakespeare mishandled *Much Ado*. He miscalculated the effect Claudio's action must have on the texture and feeling of a play that was intended to be different from the one he ended up with. *All's Well*, on the contrary, is all of a piece. Bertram's unsatisfactoriness is an aspect, albeit an important aspect, of a world that displays much that is unsatisfactory apart from his own behaviour in it.

The contrast is clear in the first scenes of both plays. *Much Ado* begins at a gallop. There is little expository matter to be divulged: we learn that Claudio has distinguished himself in Don Pedro's service and that Benedick, who has attached himself to Claudio, has acquired the habit of entering into a battle of wits with Beatrice. In the space of little more than three hundred lines the gallant hero has returned from the wars and accepted Leonato's hospitality; Benedick and Beatrice have demonstrated their tactics in the 'merry war' between them; Claudio has fallen in love with Hero and communicated this fact to Benedick and Don Pedro; and Don Pedro has volunteered to woo Hero on Claudio's behalf. All but the last forty lines of the scene are in prose, which is sprightly, elegant and obviously very pleased with itself. The speech between Leonato and the messenger at the opening is dignified but not heavy. The messenger is a practised rhetorician, squeezing into his minuscule part a good measure of Euphuistic antithesis (see my chapter of *Love's Labour's Lost*) and jingling word play. Leonato catches his partiality for puns in the speech about 'kind' and 'kindness', demonstrating that merriment, and the verbal dexterity that goes with it, are not the prerogative of the young. At the same time he leads us into the centrepiece of the scene, Beatrice's comments on Benedick and the opening skirmish between the two young people. In other words, Benedick and Beatrice set the tone, which is one of light-hearted, unimposing raillery. Beatrice is mainly responsible for carrying this forward up to the entrance of Don Pedro and his men. Then Benedick takes over. He dominates Claudio in an interval which is given over to Claudio's confession of his love for

Hero. Claudio has to wait for Benedick's exit before he can move into the centre of the stage. Then, his brief discussion with Don Pedro limps along in an indifferent blank verse which does little to divert our attention from the superior stage presence of the man who has just left it. In the next important scene, II, i, Benedick and Beatrice are once again, by turns, in command.

In short, Messina is represented as a place in which domestic civility, aggressive wit tempered with good manners, intellectual and verbal resource, and romantic attachments between the sexes jostle together quite comfortably, as a rule. I shall be discussing the way things become less comfortable later in the play. For the moment I want to do no more than establish the mood of the opening, and I think what I have said is a fair description of it.

By contrast, the first scene of *All's Well* is grave and deliberate. The language the characters speak appears only reluctantly to release the plot from the constraint of its heavy rhythms and retarding syntax. Helena's history almost disappears beneath the weight of abstraction Lafeu and the Countess of Rousillon bring to bear on their memories of it. Helena herself, before she is left alone on the stage, appears as little more than a peg on which to hang disquisitions about virtue and inheritance. I shall quote a passage from each play to make clear the point that I am making. This is Beatrice, in *Much Ado*, talking about Benedick's reputation as a lady-killer:

> He set up his bills here in Messina, and challeng'd Cupid at the flight; and my uncle's fool, reading the challenge, sub-scrib'd for Cupid, and challeng'd him at the bird-bolt. I pray you, how many hath he kill'd and eaten in these wars? But how many hath he kill'd? For, indeed, I promised to eat all of his killing.

The picture of Benedick's character is painted entirely with meta-phor – bills, Cupids, subscriptions, bird-bolts. The syntax is direct and forceful, the subordinate phrases brief and put in the most obvious places, the links between the principal clauses simple – usually unassuming co-ordinations. Compare this passage from *All's Well*, in which the Countess offers Lafeu her opinion of Helena's character:

> I have those hopes of her good, that her education promises;

her dispositions she inherits, which makes fair gifts fairer; for where an unclean mind carries virtuous qualities, there commendations go with pity – they are virtues and traitors too. In her they are the better for their simpleness, she derives her honesty, and achieves her goodness.

The style is bare of metaphorical ornament. It makes its point by a combination of ratiocinative grammar, which compresses the argument just within the boundaries of sense, and abstract vocabulary. The 'gifts' and 'traitors' do not have the substantial presence of the 'bills' and 'bird-bolts' in Beatrice's speech. Further the Countess is in no hurry to make her point about Helena. She weaves into the middle of her speech a long parenthesis on inherited dispositions, which trails sluggishly through four subsidiary clauses before the speech returns to Helena with 'In her . . .'. Helena disappears between the interstices of the Countess's syntax. As we shall see, her own powers of expression may have acquired their character from an intense desire to establish herself as a person in a play that keeps depriving persons of those qualities that do most to promote the establishment of an individual life.

The 'skirmish of wit' between Benedick and Beatrice is replaced by the banter between Helena and Parolles on the subject of virginity. Parolles is not a man to be accused of abstracting the idea of virginity from the presence of virginity in real-life virgins, and he gets some distasteful humour out of his pies, porridge and French withered pears. But the argument is a persistent and continuous one. The subject of their argument doesn't change with the change in tactics of the people who are arguing. Apart from this, Helena doesn't stand up to Parolles as Beatrice does to Benedick. For half the scene she gives Parolles his head. When she does offer her own views on the subject they are scarcely directed towards him. The tone and phrasing of her speech, coupled with the fact that it has transformed itself from prose to verse, make it clear to the audience that she is communicating with no one but herself. Once again a transaction between people on the stage has given way to something more inward, more generally speculative, in a sense more undramatic.

This is one way of suggesting the principal difference between the two plays. The action of *Much Ado* darts across a surface of witty conversation, vivid events, rapid changes of fortune among the characters. At least that is what it looks like from the vantage point of the end of I, i, or even II, ii; though as I hope to show we may be disabused of these simple notions as we move onward into the middle and later scenes. But, from the outset, *All's Well* is weighed down by a mysterious incapacity or unwillingness to issue in action. The scene at the French court, which follows the one we have been looking at, does nothing to improve matters. The characters in *Much Ado* – young and old – seem to be impelled forward by a vigorously youthful spirit of action and adventure. Those of *All's Well* seem to withdraw themselves from the strains of dramatic identity. They retire behind the peculiar language they have evolved to set themselves at a distance from themselves. Helena's struggle to free herself from the verbal no less than the temperamental restraints she has had imposed on her, meet with a mixture of success and failure. That is a matter to be taken up a little later. First let us look at how the heroes cope with their very different conditions of theatrical existence.

★　　★　　★　　★　　★

It has been said of *Much Ado about Nothing* that the poetic element is absent and that the dramatic and novelistic elements are unusually strong. The point being made is not the simple one that much of this play is written in prose. Most of Shakespeare's plays in the last years of the sixteenth century have a lot of prose in them. Nor is it that the organisation of the time scheme counts for more than it usually does in the comedies, though it is true that the timing of the Watch's discovery of Don John's plot is calculated to heighten dramatic suspense in a way that is unfamiliar in most of the earlier comedies, and will continue to be so in *As You Like It* (which immediately follows *Much Ado*). I think what the critic was getting at is that although, as I have said, the clever raillery of Beatrice and Benedick colours our initial response to the play and affects our expectations as to what sort of a play it will be (what tone and atmosphere it will have), the dramatic thrust of the play is provided by Claudio, in his changing attitudes to Hero and his facile capitulation to Don John's dastardly plot. The scenes between Benedick and Beatrice, on the one hand, and those between Don Pedro, Claudio and Hero on the other, are quite different in feeling. There is a difference in the way the characters express themselves and in the way they encourage the audience to take notice of them. We discovered how abrupt the change in dramatic effect can be in our brief survey of the first scene. When Benedick leaves Don Pedro and Claudio alone on the stage his absence is felt in the diminished range of tonal resource in the speech of the characters who remain. It is not simply a matter of the shift from prose into verse. Claudio's prose speech, especially where it is not delivered to Benedick, is as flat as his verse is here. The difference lies more in the relationship between the words that are spoken and the characters who are speaking them.

Beatrice and Benedick use words as bright shiny counters in a game of wit. Their object in displaying them is not to convey information or to announce intentions or to express themselves in any obvious or direct way. It is to dazzle the person spoken to, or to neutralise the dazzle created by the words that person might make use of in his turn. So Beatrice and Benedick stand at a distance from their own words and the attitudes, wishes and intentions they signify. Language is a brilliant camouflage behind which they protect a valuable privacy, an enclave of discretion in the public world from which they do not wish to retire but into which they do not wish to be totally absorbed. For Claudio and Hero, words are quite simply the outward expression of their inner feelings. For a moment, at III, i (the overhearing scene), Hero's verse reveals an otherwise untypical vein of colloquial wit. Elsewhere it is a colourless medium through which the mere outlines of her desires and intentions travel like spectres from line to line. Bertram's language is uniformly utilitarian, whether in verse or prose. The verse is unpretentiously pedestrian, given over almost entirely to the object of moving the story forward. The prose on occasion apes Benedick's witty antitheses, but it is patently an imitation. As such it secures little respect and provokes no amusement. Basically Claudio and Hero are servants, not masters, of the language they use. What they *say* they are is a fitting, is an adequate description of *what* they are. This is unusual in Shakespeare. Normally he allows his major characters (and many of his minor ones) some portion of the privacy I was talking about *à propos* Benedick and Beatrice. There is a space between the language and the person who speaks the language, and in that space the person can indulge a certain freedom of manoeuvre, striking at words from an oblique angle. This protects him from any simplifying identifications with the words he uses. Claudio and Hero are so identified. Their language is workaday, threadbare. It lacks mystery and surprise. It is unenigmatic. And their personalities are consistent with the qualities of the language they use. They too are unmysterious, unenigmatic, uninteresting. But they are at the centre of the play. So we have to be interested in them. The strain they impose on our capacity to be interested accounts for a great deal of the unsatisfactoriness we feel about *Much Ado*.

Claudio's language does not encourage us to look for any half lights or mysteries in his character. What there is of him is all on the surface, in his professed inclinations, intentions, likes and dislikes. When we look at the surface, what do we find? I submit that we find certain traits of character which, by their very nature as much as by the train of events they set in motion, bid fair to destroy the civilised and urbane, if rather aggressive, tone which Benedick and Beatrice manage to establish in the first two acts of the play. Claudio is no Leander to Hero's unclassical Hero (Marlowe and Chapman's *Hero and Leander* was published in 1598: this would not have escaped Shakespeare's attention; nor would the irony of the identification of the legendary hero and heroine with all that was most devout and steadfast in love). Indeed Claudio's atrocious behaviour towards Hero in the church scene is but the tip of the ubiquitous iceberg – an awkward image which I could not resist, suggesting as it does in the context the chilly, submerged nine-tenths of Claudio's glacial disposition (though it contrives to be tepid too). He accepts Don John's story immediately –'O mischief strangely thwarting' (the mischief appears to be Hero's, not John's) – only awaiting the ocular proof critics find Othello so uncouth in demanding, after a much lengthier temptation than Claudio undergoes here. His attitude towards women throughout is more mercenary than that of any other Shakespearean hero: returning from the wars he is struck by Hero's beauty, but wants to know if Leonato has any son to leave his money to before he allows Don Pedro to press his suit; and when he is due to marry Antonio's spurious daughter Leonato is canny enough to realise he will want to know that 'she alone is heir to both of us'. Oh good, says Claudio, in that case 'Which is the lady I must seize

upon?' His idea of doing penance for his scandalous treatment
of Hero is expressed in terms that suggest he intends to rape
her cousin. Long before we arrive at the church scene, Benedick
and Beatrice have been transformed into players of the 'interim'
Don Pedro had referred to at the end of II, i. The Claudio plot has
nudged them to one side, and indeed their contribution to the
main action of the play is negligible. Beatrice's celebrated order
to Benedick to kill Claudio does nothing to thrust him into the
plot again. When we see him next, joking with Margaret, he
appears to have forgotten all about it. Beatrice's entrance, which
reminds him of his promise, soon turns his mind to more interesting matters. And in the next scene all is made good before
Hero's tomb.

Benedick and Beatrice did not appear in Shakespeare's source,
a story by Bandello. But since 1663 the play seems to have been
famous by virtue of their appearance in it (Charles I called it
Benedick and Beatrice, and it is not difficult to imagine what
Restoration players would have made of the parts). But it is
impossible to ignore the fact that though the tone of the play is
established by Benedick and Beatrice, the plot is dominated by
Claudio; and the further the plot develops, the more seriously is
the comic tone undermined. It is a matter of strength capitulating
to weakness in a situation where weakness occupies the greater
expanse of playing time. Why did Shakespeare devote so much
time and effort to the portrait of such a commonplace young
man? I think it is a matter of muddled intentions.

Shakespeare's plays are full of *non sequiturs*, contradictions
and loose ends. None is so replete with them than *Much Ado*.
Some are obviously no more than signs of hasty composition or
inadequate revision. In II, ii, for example, editors are hard put
to it to provide reasonable explanations of why Borachio should
think it is such a good idea for Margaret, pretending to be Hero,
to call him Claudio. You have to be very ingenious to show
how putting this into practice would be likely to pull the wool
over Claudio's eyes. Then again, editors differ as to who is
speaking to Margaret in the mask scene (II, i). All the early
editors of the play read Benedick. But Benedick has evinced no
interest in Margaret. In any case this is a very formal scene in
which the conversation of one pair of 'lovers' is rapidly followed
by that of another. Each of the principal characters is given one,

and only one, opportunity to usurp the centre of the stage; and Benedick has his conversation (appropriately, with Beatrice) ten lines further down the page. The Alexander text, along with most others, gets over the problem by substituting Balthasar for Benedick. I think there are good reasons for substituting Borachio instead. But whatever we think of the alternative readings, we have to admit that here is another, not very important, example of Shakespeare (probably – it could have been the printer of the Quarto) fudging the text. There are several other minor instances.

The baffling little scene that follows i, i raises much more important issues. I believe that if we can find out what it is doing there, we shall be able to explain what makes *Much Ado* as a whole unsatisfactory. We shall also be able to explain the otherwise inexplicable importance of Claudio's role in the play. There is no very obvious justification for this scene. Most producers cut it, because it clutters the action with unnecessary confusions. You will remember that in it Antonio, Hero's uncle, tells Leonato how, 'walking in a thick-pleach'd alley in mine orchard', Don Pedro and Claudio were overheard by one of his men. He thought they were discussing Don Pedro's love for Hero. In fact it was Claudio's love for her they were discussing. Antonio's son makes a speechless and altogether unnecessary appearance in the scene. Later Claudio is informed that Antonio has no children apart from the Hero-substitute he is supposed to be marrying. There can be no doubt that the scene adds nothing to the play. Nothing comes of it. We are led from this scene to consider other matters that nothing comes of, but that nonetheless promise confusion of an altogether different kind from the confusion that actually occurs.

I am referring to Don Pedro's wooing of Hero. He has told Claudio:

I know we shall have revelling to-night;
I will assume thy part in some disguise,
And tell fair Hero I am Claudio,
And in her bosom I'll unclasp my heart,
And take her hearing prisoner with the force
And strong encounter of my amorous tale.

So far as we can see, the Prince has no ulterior motive. His sole concern is to help Claudio win Hero's hand. After Don

Pedro has explained his tactics to Claudio, there appears the little scene we have just been discussing. Then Don John hears about the plot. But it looks as if he genuinely doesn't believe his brother is wooing on Claudio's behalf. 'Sure my brother is amorous on Hero' he tells Borachio, in circumstances which detract not a jot from his sincerity. When he tells Claudio, under the pretence that he has mistaken his identity, that this is so, Claudio immediately believes him, just as he immediately believes Don John about Hero's infidelity later on. ''Tis certain so;' he says, 'the Prince woos for himself', and there follows the only passage of real poetry he speaks in the whole play. Not surprisingly it is in the theme of constancy in friendship and its betrayal in the 'office and affairs of love' – the theme of the sonnets, in fact. But no matter. Don John's perfunctory stratagem comes to nothing, as it was bound to do. Don Pedro and Leonato tell Claudio it has all been a big mistake, and the young couple are engaged.

Why is so much of the first two acts taken up with these issueless mistakings? Several reasons have been advanced. Don John has to be seen to fail once, so that we shall expect him to fail a second time in the (only slightly) more serious plot against Hero. The action of *Much Ado* takes the form of a series of misunderstandings, usually springing from an over-hearing of one kind or another. The misunderstandings over Don Pedro's wooing of Hero are a suitable prelude to the later misunderstandings between Claudio and Hero, and Benedick and Beatrice. These seem to me to be lame excuses for an undeniable clumsiness in the construction of the plot. After all, a great deal is lost through the presence of these scenes, and this has to be set against the very questionable gains I have suggested. Why should Claudio accept that Antonio's daughter is his only child? More seriously, why does Don John remain in favour with the Prince after transparently deceiving Claudio over his intentions towards Hero? Why does Claudio believe him a second time when he has been proved a liar the first? These *non sequiturs* and confusions add up to something more than the usual Shakespearean carelessness over the details of his plots. They point in the direction of a strangely ambivalent attitude on Shakespeare's part towards the possibilities of the material he is working with. Whilst these scenes and parts of scenes add nothing to the play we have, they would have added a great deal to another play Shakespeare did not write but that he could have written from the same source – given his habit of tinkering with those parts of the source he didn't happen to like very much. In the source there is no Don Pedro figure. Critics have adduced from Shakespeare's addition of Don Pedro to his own *dramatis personae* that he intended to do his best to justify the way Claudio treats Hero. If the admirable Prince believes his wicked brother and thinks Hero gets no more than she deserves, how can we blame young Claudio for believing and thinking the same? But we could look at it another way. In the source, Claudio is not so young as he is represented in *Much Ado*. And he is of a much higher station in life, which emphasises the social gap between himself and Hero. In fact he is much more like Don Pedro than Claudio. One could revise the usual account of the genesis of the play and say that, in terms of character and station, Claudio, not Don Pedro, is Shakespeare's addition. Then Don Pedro's supposed wooing for himself in the play becomes the same thing as his actual wooing for himself in the source. Shakespeare has split his source hero down the middle and in doing so landed himself with an addition to the plot which carried more serious overtones than anything he found in the Italian.

Borachio explains his plot to Don John in the following terms. He will adduce proof enough 'to misuse the Prince, to vex Claudio, to undo Hero, and kill Leonato'. So far as I can remember, no other villain in a Shakespearean comedy behaves as villainously as this. But in a tragedy he does. I mean in *Othello*. Accept Shakespeare's vestigial but still creative interest in Don Pedro as next of kin to the hero in the source, along with the occasional depression of Claudio's role which is its consequence – so that Claudio (called Don Pedro) is the go-between and Don Pedro (called Claudio) the lover – and you have a situation which is potentially the one we find in *Othello*. Don Pedro, the Prince, is Othello; Claudio is Cassio; Hero is Desdemona; and Leonato is Brabantio. Iago (Don John) intends, initially, to misuse, not to kill, Othello; to vex Cassio; to undo Desdemona. In the process it so happens that Brabantio dies, though I concede I should be stretching the point if I said Iago killed him. So those little awkwardnesses that impede the forward movement of the main plot, combined with aspects of the main plot itself (especially when considered alongside the source), tend in the direction of a tragic action. This never fully discloses itself, but it lies close enough to the surface to depress the comic design and thwart any movement towards light-heartedness or exuberance. Benedick and Beatrice struggle in vain against this tendency. They remain delightful in themselves. But they cannot prevent the tragic potential of the play (which Shakespeare must have sensed, even as he saw that his hero was unable to release it) from compromising the gaiety of the opening atmosphere and setting. A hard deposit of unpleasantness crystallises around Claudio and sinks the centre of the play. The weight that sinks it is the weight of Shakespeare's unrealisable intentions. The play does not grin, but bears it.

*   *   *   *   *

The plot of *All's Well that Ends Well* is more like that of a folk-tale than is usual in the comedies. The event that sets it in motion, Helena's curing of the King of France, is a version of one typical ingredient of folk-tale. The apparently impossible task Bertram challenges Helena to perform is a version of another. The main action, the love of a poor physician's daughter for a handsome courtier, is a traditional feature of fairy-tale. But the world of the play does not reinforce this important aspect of the plot. In fact it seems to go out of its way to do the opposite. The plot is fantastic, extravagant, improbable. The world of the play is sceptical, inquisitive, dryly philosophical. The combination of an improbable plot and a brooding, reflective and philosophical atmosphere creates a distinct sense of unease in most audiences. It is difficult to respond to the play as a whole because in each scene the method of presentation tends to obscure the 'shape' of whatever is being presented. Consequently audiences, and readers, become restive. They have difficulty in adjusting to the way the language the characters speak goes against the grain of the action in which they are seen to be speaking it. Let me offer an example.

Act II, scene iii brings before us the conclusion of the first episode from folk-tale. Helena has cured the King. She now claims her reward: the choice of a husband from the ranks of the assembled courtiers. The choosing is done in a ritualistic manner, with each lord singled out for comment in turn. It comes as no surprise that Helena's choice finally alights on Bertram. It comes as no surprise, either, that Bertram recoils from the obligation to marry someone he has never thought of as anything other than a family servant. 'A poor physician's daughter my wife! Disdain/Rather corrupt me ever!' is his comment on the business. Quite in keeping with the folk-tale substance of the scene. But the King's reply breaks the spell:

'Tis only title thou disdain'st in her, the which
I can build up. Strange is it that our bloods,
Of colour, weight, and heat, pour'd all together,
Would quite confound distinction, yet stand off
In differences so mighty. If she be
All that is virtuous – save what thou dislik'st,
A poor physician's daughter – thou dislik'st
Of virtue for the name; but do not so.
From lowest place when virtuous thing proceed,
The place is dignified by th'doer's deed;
Where great additions swell's, and virtue none,
It is a dropsied honour. Good alone
Is good without a name. Vileness is so:
The property by what it is should go,
Not be the title. She is young, wise, fair,
In these to nature she's immediate heir;
And these breed honour. That is honour's scorn
Which challenges itself as honour's born
And is not like the sire. Honours thrive
When rather from our acts we them derive
Than our fore-goers. The mere word's a slave,
Debauch'd on every tomb, on every grave
A lying trophy; and as oft is dumb
Where dust and damn'd oblivion is the tomb
Of honour'd bones indeed. What should be said?
If thou canst like this creature as a maid,
I can create the rest. Virtue and she
Is her own dower; honour and wealth from me.

Helena and Bertram retire into the background of the play whilst the foreground is occupied by this leisurely disquisition on virtue, honour and the nature of the good.

Most of the King's utterances are gravely generalised. They look like aphorisms that have lost much of their sharpness through over-use and a tendency towards sententiousness in the man who speaks them. Here they are impassioned as well as philosophical, especially near the end where the imagery becomes more profuse and expressive. This imagery is worth looking into. Much of the speech is made up of abstractions, as befits its reflective and speculative character. But is it not apparent that the King allows certain images into his speech which have nothing to do with his argument but arise naturally from his personal situation – that of an ageing man who has just been cured of a serious illness? These images, of death and decay, may have been triggered off by Bertram's earlier reference to corruption. The King's description of 'bloods' is grossly physical, characterised by colour, weight and heat rather than by any moral qualities, and 'pour'd altogether' before 'standing off' in a less substantial way. Honour is 'dropsied' when pompous titles 'swell' us. The speech ends with those images of death – tombs, graves, dust and honoured bones – that clamour for our attention by virtue of the rhetorical force with which they are fused together to create a single, powerful expression of mortality.

The style of the King's speech is at odds with the dramatic circumstances that have brought it into being. That is not the only peculiarity of this part of the scene. The moral of the speech is that it is important to distinguish between virtue and honour. Honour is the homage power pays to virtue, in the sense that he who is virtuous is deserving of honour and the ability to bestow honour belongs to the rich and powerful. But the rich and powerful are not always impartial in their gifts, and virtue is not always easily discovered. Also, honour tends to attach itself to rank as well as, or in place of, virtue. So honour is frequently suspect and virtue unrewarded. All this the King fully understands. The upshot of his speech is therefore not surprisingly to tell Bertram that he will put his principles into practice. Helena is already virtuous. All that remains is for him to bestow on her the honour that should be the outward form of virtue. This is consistent with everything he has said on the subject. But when Bertram insists he is still not satisfied and Helena says she is prepared to withdraw her claim on him, the King strikes a different note. Now, he says, 'My honour's at the stake, which to defeat,/I must produce my power.' The man who spent his first long speech scrupulously defining the properties of honour and virtue, spends his second threatening one of the insubordinate members of his court with the arbitrary withdrawal of honour, and confusing honour with virtue in his description of his own position.

What has happened is that the folk-tale has created some unforeseen problems. The King is supposed to be wise, the girl virtuous, the young man ungrateful. But, when the folk-tale is expanded into its present dramatic form, some of its features are magnified and the moral pattern of the whole situation begin to look more complex than might initially have been expected. Shakespeare does not do what we probably suppose he ought to have done: he does not underplay the awkwardness of the situation he has produced. Instead he goes out of his way to emphasise it. So the King, addressing Helena before she picks over the marriage market, draws attention to the arbitrariness of his power and the unenviable situation the courtiers have been placed in (in the folk-tale it wouldn't have been unenviable because everyone, except the naughty hero, would have been bound to love the physician's beautiful daughter) by announcing that in making her 'frank election', 'Thou hast power to choose, and they none to forsake.' There follows Bertram's excessive expression of distaste for what the King supposes he is obliged to do; then the King's speech on honour and virtue; then his angry threats, which have the effect merely of forcing Bertram into lies and prevarication. The emphasis throughout falls on the very human and realistic reactions of the characters to an intolerable situation. But the situation would not have been intolerable if the folk-tale elements had been as prominent in the tone and characterisation of the play as they are in its plot.

In spite of the King's contradictory behaviour in this scene, on the whole he is presented as being an admirable man. But his admirable qualities do not enable him to do very much, to affect the outcome of the drama. His threats to Bertram are empty. Bertram simply runs away to Florence and enlists in the wars. His promise to Helena is equally fruitless. He does not have the power to force Bertram into a marriage of inconvenience. This quality of powerlessness, of a mellow wisdom which does not possess the strength to back up its (rather gloomy) convictions, is widespread among the older characters. The King's speeches about his friendship with Bertram's father in I, ii are the most eloquent expressions of it; but it is shared by the Countess and Lafeu – both well-meaning and intelligent people, of mature years, but incapable of exerting themselves to *do* anything about the unhappy state of affairs over which they find themselves presiding. The characters who exert themselves most are the young, and they have been described by the King (quoting Bertram's father) as:

> . . . younger spirits, whose apprehensive senses
> All but new things disdain; whose judgments are
> Mere fathers of their garments; whose constancies
> Expire before their fashions . . .

If what he says is true, *All's Well that Ends Well*, along with other problem comedies of about the same date, marks a break with the earlier Shakespearean practice of representing the young (especially the young women) as not only more vital than their elders, but also more wise.

Bertram seems determined to place himself in the harshest critical light. He shares Claudio's horror of the girl who loves him, with the difference that there is not even a wicked plot afoot to afford him the ghost of an excuse. Some critics do try to find excuses for him. He is young, he has not created the circumstances which now bear so heavily on him, he has never given Helena the slightest encouragement to suppose he loves her. All of this is true. But the absence of a plot and the emphasis that is placed on Bertram's sincere, unmanipulated attitude to Helena predispose the audience to scrutinise his behaviour more carefully than was the case with Claudio. Claudio's deception by Don John and Borachio diverted the audience's attention from his own character towards the suspense of the plot. Here there is no suspense, nothing for Bertram to find out before it is too late. What suspense there is attaches to Helena: the audience wants to know how she is going to satisfy the apparently impossible conditions Bertram has insisted she shall meet before she can be his wife in deed as well as in name. The result of this scrutiny of Bertram's behaviour is that he makes an even poorer showing than Claudio did. Not because he does not want to marry Helena – that is understandable, in spite of the bias (in her favour) of the underlying folk-tale; but because the way he goes about escaping from her is so outrageously ill-mannered.

All's Well is a play in which bad manners un-make the man. Bertram has not had much of a chance to reveal his character before he is called on to react to the King's command at II, iii. He has spoken very little, and what he has spoken has been utterly conventional. The only thing he has told us about himself is that he values his freedom and fears he is about to lose it. At least this is what I take to be the implication of his first speech: 'I must attend his majesty's command, to whom I am now in ward, ever-more in subjection.' Almost as soon as he has arrived at the court he finds that his worst fears are about to be justified. He is to be forced to marry a servant. His immediate reaction to the King's command is difficult to gauge with accuracy because he has two replies: one of them long and gracious, the other short and curt ('I take her hand'). So far he has done nothing to disgrace himself. No one could blame him for his chagrin and sense of outrage over Helena. His submission to the King's demands, in spite of his own strong inclination to disobey them, may be admirable.

From the moment he returns to the stage at the end of the same scene our attitude is bound to change. The streak of self-pity ('Undone, and forfeited to cares for ever!') is not unexpected; nor is it altogether inappropriate. But it goes hand in hand with very much less attractive expressions of an ingrained petulance that begins to disclose itself to us as Bertram's most fundamental characteristic. He insists on making the worst of a bad job. 'Although before the solemn priest I have sworn/I will not bed her.' He emphasises the most unpleasant aspects of his behaviour at the expense of those that would, quite rightly, earn him some sympathy. He announces his decision to go to the wars in terms that stress the fact that he is running away *from* difficulties of one kind rather than running *towards* those of another. Worst of all, he tells Parolles he will 'write to the king/That which I durst not speak', i.e. he will sneak away without so much as a word to the guardian he is afraid to face. The sting is not in what he decides to do, or not to do, but in the manner in which he pro-claims those decisions. It is not wrong – on any fair-minded and objective assessment of his situation – for him to refuse to con-summate a marriage contracted on such questionable terms. But it is, to say the least, churlish of him to dwell on the contrast between the solemnity of the religious service and the reductive terminology of the question to bed her or not to bed her. And it is more than churlish of him to deceive Helena in the fulsome manner he assumes at II, v. It is not wrong of him, either, to flee the court in secret, since the King has previously told him that if he should refuse to marry his protégée he will loose upon him both his revenge and hate 'without all terms of pity'. What one objects to is his insistence on not doing what he 'durst' not do, a sort of wallowing in his cowardice.

There is not much to be said in Parolles' favour, but his verdict on Bertram – 'a foolish, idle boy, but for all that very ruttish' – isn't so very wide of the mark. We have to wait for the Florentine scenes to discover his ruttishness. There his good taste in selecting Diana to inflict it on is unaccountable (he doesn't seem to have any inkling of her value, supposing her to be 'a common gamester to the camp' at V, iii). His folly, idleness and callow youth, however, are evident wherever we turn after the second act. In a way his character, unpleasant as it is, is too slight to support some of the charges made against it. I have already mentioned the King's angry responses during the court scene. Helena's exclamation at IV, iv is even more to the point. Bertram's intercourse with her the night before, when he supposed she was Diana in a whimsical mood, calls forth a bitter homily of the duplicity of the male sex which Bertram seems too much of a worm to have warranted. Mention of 'saucy trusting of the cozen'd thoughts' defiling the pitchy night, and lust playing with what it loathes, summons up the proleptic spectre of Angelo in *Measure for Measure*, an older man, more practised in deceit, whose perverse passions make this kind of language entirely appropriate when it appears in the later play. Bertram, though, is too facile to deserve it. His duplicities are lent an evil grandeur they are too flimsy to sustain.

Bertram is an anti-hero in the tradition of Proteus and Claudio. What, then, of the heroine he treats so badly? Helena shares her most conspicuous characteristic with most of her sister heroines in the other comedies. This is her *activity*. Hero, in *Much Ado*, was strangely inactive. Since the plot required that her crucial act was to faint, and then remain as dead during the climax of the play, she could hardly be blamed for this. In any case, Beatrice made up for her lack of activity, with interest. It was Beatrice who was

most like the typical Shakespearean comic heroine – Julia, Rosalind, Viola, and the others (I shall have more to say about this in
chapter 10). But Helena shares with Isabella in *Measure for
Measure* a complication within the type. It is not the same complication, but it has a similar result. In both cases the *object* of
the heroine's activity deprives her of the audience's usual sympathetic response. The role she has to play, again in conformation
with the outline of the folk-tale, causes us to dislike her: because
unlike Claudio, the man she claims she loves has done nothing to
encourage her to pursue him; and because, unlike Proteus, he has
not broken a pledge or an understanding that has given her sufficient grounds for supposing she enjoys a special relationship with
him. Helena is a fully fledged development, in psychological
terms, of her less conspicuous namesake in *A Midsummer Night's
Dream*. Like that other Helena she sets her sights on a man who
has no interest in her whatsoever, and she allows nothing to stand
in the way of her merciless pursuit of him. The difference is that
this Helena needs no fairies to streak her victim's eyes with magic
juices. She has nothing but her single-minded devotion to the
pursuit and her ingenious intelligence to help her. But these prove
more than enough to run Bertram to ground.

Yet Helena's progress through the play is more interesting than
this summary of her character would lead one to believe. Some
critics feel it is wrong to look at her too closely because she should
be accepted as a fairy-tale heroine and no more. One of them
goes so far as to say that he will give her no attention because he
takes her for granted, 'which is the right way with her'. (The
critic is A. P. Rossiter in *Angel with Horns.*) This is surely part of
an over-simplified account of the play. It is a fairy-tale, if you
like. It is also a sceptical analysis of certain virtues, which include
honour, knowledge and loyalty. Helena's origins as a folk-tale
heroine do not absolve her from playing her part in this analysis.
Indeed the analysis proceeds by way of making the folk-tale submit to several realistic tests which detract not a little from its sim-
plicity and uniformity of character, as we have seen. Helena's
central position in the folk-tale carries with it the obligation of
focusing several of the moral issues thrown up by the analytical
method of the play. This I think she does by changing her role in
it after the second act. As Bertram's character becomes more
and more prominent, Helena's fades more and more into the

background. Although she continues to push the plot forward, she does so less as a vividly apprehended personality and more as a stock property of the fairy-tale she spent most of Acts I and II outgrowing.

I owe this point to Barbara Everett, in her provocative introduction to the Penguin edition of *All's Well*. She points out that unlike Shakespeare's other comic heroines Helena is not a 'steady-state character'. In the first half of the play she is always evolving from one state of theatrical existence to another, 'coming into being as a character, just as – in naturalistic terms – she is coming into being as a person'. Interestingly, she is also unlike other comic heroines in being given the privilege of soliloquy. In the first scene she has two quite long and involved soliloquies, and I have already commented on the way in her 'conversation' with Parolles she seems intensely self-involved and discrete, not really a participant in a dramatic exchange at all. I am inclined, therefore, to agree with Barbara Everett that Helena is presented to us in these early scenes of *All's Well* as a character in process of formation, gradually assuming a personality as she 'puts a body into wishing well', to use her own words at I, i, 177. As she painfully gropes towards the plan she is going to put into operation in the French court, the 'she' that gropes towards it comes into more and more substantial existence. Then in the later scenes it fades away. Mrs Everett has an explanation for this as well. 'Helena', she says, 'has discovered energies in herself to initiate the long advance into activity that is her propulsion of the plot, until she becomes (some would say) *mere* activity, capable of managing the plot and of nothing else.'

I think this is too ingenious. It is claimed that Helena's self-analysis in the soliloquies reveals to her the self of a folk-tale heroine, which allows her to come up with the plan to cure the King – just what a folk-tale heroine is supposed to do. Later, when she sees she cannot trap Bertram into a consummated marriage on her own terms, she puts her knowledge of her literary identity to good use by accepting her role as an object, to be used by Bertram in what he falsely (though in a deeper sense perhaps correctly) supposes is an assertion of freedom. This strikes me as being a Nabokovian solution of what is really an insoluble problem, because there is no getting away from the fact that the last three acts of *All's Well* are *as a whole* inferior to the first two. It cannot be a coincidence that in them Shakespeare has developed the 'mechanical' folk-tale plot at the expense of the questioning, reflective poetry that had so much complicated our responses to the earlier scenes. Nothing is gained by Helena's transforming herself into the folk-tale heroine she was discovering herself to be in I, i, except a means of concluding the play. Bertram would have to make more of his release into liberty than in fact he does (to tell the truth he sounds no more sincere in his recantation than he did in II, iii). For it follows from Mrs Everett's interpretation that the more Helena converts herself into an object, the more of a subject, a free subject with a developed personality, she causes Bertram to be. But Bertram remains obstinately null, no more convincing in his second marriage to Helena than he was in his first. I think it is more consistent with the facts to accept that Shakespeare lost interest in what he was doing from Act III onwards. Significantly when we return to the court at v, iii the language resumes its earlier peculiar withdrawn effect, and the reconciliation scene is much better than its equivalent in *Measure for Measure*. The King, especially, makes much of his elegiac, sententious utterances. Shakespeare's real sympathy at this time seems to have remained with the aged and inactive, however compromised they were by the tale they had to tell. His interest faded when they left the stage.

8
As You Like It

As You Like It may not be the most popular, but it is the most perfect of Shakespeare's comedies. For a long time it was popular too. It was often played in the eighteenth century (in the first half in Charles Johnson's adaptation *Love in the Forest*) and both at that time and in the early nineteenth century many famous actors and actresses excelled in the parts of Touchstone, Jaques and Rosalind. Macklin played Touchstone. Kemble, Macready and Phelps played Jaques. Rosalind was played by Peg Woffington and Mrs Siddons and, before the last war in this century, by Edith Evans and Sybil Thorndike. The popularity of *As You Like It* has declined with the increased interest in problem comedies like *Measure for Measure* and late romances like *The Winter's Tale*. In other words mid-twentieth-century audiences are often unsympathetic to the genre of romantic comedy to which this play so pre-eminently belongs. There is not even the bitter-sweet flavour of the end of *Twelfth Night* to recommend it. Instead the lovers all return from the forest to the comfort of the court, leaving behind them the only two characters – Duke Frederick and Jaques – who find they can benefit from the solitude of Arden. Arden itself is a problem. For it reminds us throughout that the action of the play takes place according to the convention of pastoral, and this convention strikes us today as artificial in the extreme.

Earlier comedies of Shakespeare had included sequences of pastoral. In *The Two Gentlemen of Verona*, *Love's Labour's Lost* and *A Midsummer Night's Dream* a pastoral scene was 'inset' as a place of healing and self-knowledge. As the plays followed one another the pastoral element became more pronounced, growing from two meagre scenes in *The Two Gentlemen of Verona* to fill out the middle acts of *A Midsummer Night's Dream*. In *As You Like It* the whole play, with the exception of the first act, is set in a pastoral landscape. More than this, it is understood to be just that by the characters who live in it. They are highly conscious of the pastoral roles they play, from the Duke in his speech on the life of exile and the uses of adversity in II, i, to Touchstone arguing with the old shepherd Corin on the pros and cons of court and country life in III, ii. In later plays Shakespeare will continue to use pastoral devices – in Act IV of *The Winter's Tale* and in *The Tempest*, where the island is a peculiar variant of pastoral landscape. Even the middle scenes of *King Lear* are inverted pastoral on the heath and in the fields near Dover, and of course the sub-plot involving Gloucester and his sons was injected into the play from the episode of the Paphlagonian King in Sir Philip Sidney's *Arcadia*. But Shakespeare never used the device more exclusively and more purely than he did here. So the first question we must ask ourselves in looking at *As You Like It* is: what was pastoral, how was the convention used and what was its purpose?

The best way I can explain it is by looking back several years to the sixth book of Edmund Spenser's romance allegory, *The Faerie Queene*. In Canto IX of this poem the hero, Sir Calidore, has entered the pastoral setting of old Meliboe and the two lovers Coridon and Pastorella. The fact that his attentions to Pastorella have done nothing to improve the already unpromising situation of the two lovers should not be allowed to detract from the sincerity of his expostulation on the virtues of the life they all live:

How much (sayd he) more happie is the state,
In which ye father here doe dwell at ease,
Leading a life so free and fortunate,
From all the tempests of these worldly seas,
Which tosse the rest in daungerous disease;
Where waves, and wreckes, and wicked enmitie
Doe them afflict, which no man can appease,
That certes I your happinesse envie,
And wishe my lot were plast in such felicitee.

Meliboe answers that this is perfectly true. He envies no one because he is content that 'having small, yet doe I not complaine/ Of want, ne wish for more it to augment'. He is taught by nature to be satisfied with what he has. There is little point in striving for more, for 'They that have much, feare much to loose thereby,/And store of cares doth follow riches store.'

In Shakespeare's play, as in Spenser's poem, little awkwardnesses like long winters and wet summers are passed over without comment. 'Here feel we not the penalty of Adam' nor of the English climate, which does put in a retrospective appearance in the Duke's speech – but the play as a whole is bathed in summer sunshine. The point is that the pastoral setting represents an idealised retreat from the affairs of the world and is used as a background to courteous disputation and 'example'. The object is to satisfy a *faux-naif* delight in romance of the kind Thomas Lodge provided in his narrative of *Rosalynde* (1590) – the story Shakespeare used as the main thread on which to hang his scenes and incidents in *As You Like It*. We can compare Sir Calidore's speech from *The Faerie Queene* or some of the speeches in *Rosalynde* itself, on the pleasures of the pastoral life, with that of the Duke at the opening of II, i.

> Now my co-mates and brothers in exile,
> Hath not old custom made this life more sweet
> Than that of painted pomp? Are not these woods
> More free from peril than the envious court?
> Here feel we not the penalty of Adam,
> The seasons' difference, as the icy fang
> And churlish chiding of the winter's wind,
> Which when it bites and blows upon my body
> Even till I shrink with cold, I smile and say
> 'This is no flattery; these are counsellors
> That feelingly persuade me what I am.'
> Sweet are the uses of adversity,
> Which like the toad, ugly and venomous,
> Wears yet a precious jewel in his head;
> And this our life, exempt from public haunt,
> Finds tongues in trees, books in the running brooks,
> Sermons in stones, and good in everything.

The lesson is the same. The difference emerges only when we put the Duke's speech back into the scene we took it from.

One of the Duke's followers, Amiens, is in complete agreement: 'I would not change it', he says. 'Happy is your grace/ That can translate the stubbornness of fortune/Into so quiet and so sweet a style.' But the Duke's reply makes us pause for thought. He suggests that they should go off and 'kill us venison'. Now it is obvious that the greenwood company must eat, and we have no need to pretend that they are vegetarians. But there is a difference between bringing meat or even shooting deer, and 'killing venison'. The verb is very direct and brutal. More so when, in obscuring his intentions with perfunctory tear for the 'poor dappled fools', he blunders into talk of 'goring' their round haunches. Bloodier and bloodier. We also prick up our ears at his reference to the forest as a 'desert city', which prepares us for Orlando's description of it a little later as a 'desert inaccessible', and an 'uncouth forest' full of 'melancholy boughs'. Part of this can be explained in terms of pathetic fallacy; part of it by the Duke's propensity to sentimentalise his misfortunes. But not all. Elsewhere there is not very much natural description, and what there is is pleasing and properly pastoral. Even the wounded stag 'sequesters' itself – much better than going to ground – 'Under an oak whose antick root peeps out/Upon a brook that brawls along this wood'. All very delightful – for the stag too, we are to suppose. 'Brawls' there is positively Keatsian. None of this should disguise the fact, however, that there is a double landscape in *As You Like It*. Before we look at the use to which it is put, let us go back to some other changes Shakespeare makes to the story he found in Lodge's romance.

The greatest change is in the plotting, or rather the lack of it. There is no complex and dynamic design of the kind we discovered in *A Midsummer Night's Dream*. It would be impossible to produce a plan of the action as I did in the case of the earlier comedy. All that happens is that Duke Frederick dislikes Duke Senior, which makes things difficult for the two girls who are their respective daughters; and Oliver dislikes Orlando, which interferes with Orlando's love for Rosalind (until Oliver himself has fallen in love with her sister). Apart from Oliver's falling in love with Celia, the pattern of relationships is fully worked out by the end of Act I, where all the groups of characters (apart from Duke Senior, who is already there) run off to the Forest of Arden. That is, the plot is virtually over by the end of Act I. It is a more extreme example of what happened in *Love's Labour's Lost*.

From Act II onwards all that happens, except for the final tying-up process that comes with the recantation of the two villains, is that the various parties meet each other, converse, and sing songs. A fair amount of wooing goes on, in the shape of a

game or a masquerade. Also, various minor characters – Touchstone, Jaques, Silvius, Phebe, Corin, Adam, Amiens and
William – move in and out of the action, having conversations,
love affairs and debates. The plot is very thin. It has no work to
do because there is no intrigue – only minor dislocations the
characters produce for themselves – to delay the necessary disclosures. All await a change of heart by Oliver and the wicked
Duke. When this comes, it comes in the most artificial way con-
ceivable. Surely deliberately so. Oliver is threatened not only by
a snake but by a lioness too, 'with udders all drawn dry', when
Orlando happens upon him and saves him from a fate worse than
pantomime. Frederick meets a good old hermit and his conver-
sion is announced to the players by a third son of Sir Roland de
Boys who hasn't received a mention up to v, iv. It is as if Shakespeare is saying: 'This thing has got to come to an end somehow.
What more appropriate than these absurd intrusions? Plot, after
all, isn't terribly important. So let's resolve it all with a cardboard
menagerie and the odd hermit who is always to be found hanging
about somewhere in pastoral.' There is no call to take matters
any more seriously than this.

The most memorable scenes in *As You Like It* have nothing to
do with the plot. Orlando's intrusion into the Duke's conversation
with Jaques at II, vii is brief and cursory. We are not concerned
with him or with Adam, whom he has left in the forest. What we
are interested in is Jaques' melancholy and the Duke's response
to it. When Orlando goes off to fetch Adam, we can sit back
again and enjoy Jaques' speech on the seven ages of man. The
debate between Corin and Touchstone in III, ii, that I have
referred to before, is rightly one of the most admired passages in
the play. It is followed by the scene in which Rosalind, disguised
as Ganymede, persuades Orlando to take her for his mistress in
rehearsing his address to her – a scene which does nothing to
resolve the plot and everything to hold it up; to substitute for it a
little game that will amuse her, and will amuse us, but will
advance the narrative not a jot. In an essay on the idea of play in
As You Like It D. J. Palmer points out that Rosalind doesn't
need her disguise after she has found both Orlando and her father
in Arden, yet she maintains it from III, i, on in spite of the fact
that one of these requirements has already been met, and the
other could be met at any time she chooses. She doesn't so

choose until v, iv, thus allowing the play to proceed. Similar scenes, in which much is done but little progress is made, are those involving Touchstone and Audrey, and Touchstone and Jaques at II, iii, and Silvius, Phebe and Rosalind at III, v. These are all conversation pieces on the absurdity of sex and the folly of courtly love. In each case either they make no contribution to the plot or they actually impede its progress.

The play develops in quite another way, in bringing together different members of different groups for purposes of dispute and argument – even going to the lengths of introducing William in Act v so as to give Touchstone a new butt to mock at during his courtship of Audrey. It is worthy of note that Touchstone doesn't meet Duke Senior until Act v, a delay that creates a new 'area' in which he and Jaques can conduct their argument. The form of *As You Like It* is therefore centrifugal – an ugly word, but the most appropriate I can find to describe this play. Characters belonging to different groups temporarily disperse and recombine talkatively with members of other groups. They are always moving outwards from their position within the group they were attached to at first to a new one at the circumference of a quite separate group. So Jaques meets Touchstone, Rosalind meets Phebe, Touchstone meets William, and each of them gets involved, in a mocking, detached sort of way, in an action which is not, and usually doesn't remain, his own. The dialogues and conversations that ensue are loosely held together by a spoof romance plot, the pivots of which take the form of wrestlers, lionesses, snakes and hermits. Neither the lionesses nor the lovers are taken terribly seriously. The lionesses, however, are absurd. At bottom, the lovers are not. Though they are treated lightly, they contrive to make a kind of sense out of the comic situation in which they are discovered. Though they are not serious in themselves, a seriousness of a kind can be made to emerge from a study of their fortunes.

Now we can return to the pastoral setting, the double landscape, and place the lovers' arguments in the context it provides for them. I noted above that this was reminiscent of *A Midsummer Night's Dream*, in two ways. First, in both plays the tangle of love affairs is unpicked in a pastoral setting – of a different kind, as the imagery makes clear, but a pastoral setting nevertheless. Second, in *A Midsummer Night's Dream* also we responded to a double landscape – according to the way that the fairies or Theseus, Bottom dreaming or Bottom awake, see it. There are two corresponding differences. In *A Midsummer Night's Dream* a great deal of the action was precipitated by supernatural agents. Here, all we have are human nature and unpersonified chances and accidents. Also, in *A Midsummer Night's Dream* whole groups of characters see the natural scene in different, often conflicting, ways; and they do so consistently, or their changes of viewpoint are explained by the different positions they occupy at different stages in the working out of the plot. In *As You Like It* responses to 'desert' or 'pastoral' are made by the same character, with no alteration in time, place or fortune to explain the change. We have a checker'd scene rather than an alternately ordered and disordered one. Seeing double is a perpetual, not a climactic, experience.

The change from the manner of *A Midsummer Night's Dream* to that of *As You Like It* is a local example of an overall change of emphasis that occurs as we move from the early through the middle comedies. I refer to the way Shakespeare chooses to deal with the subject of romantic love. In the early comedies, the parts for the ladies were relatively small, especially those for the adult ladies, those who knew what they were about. The love affairs between Proteus and Julia and Valentine and Silvia in *Two Gentlemen of Verona* were subordinated to the theme of friendship as it was exemplified by the relationship between Proteus and Valentine. The French ladies in *Love's Labour's Lost* had less to say for themselves than their male counterparts. And Portia, in *The Merchant of Venice*, had to withdraw behind the caskets until Act IV of that play. As a result, most of the speeches about love were spoken by the men and (because of the immaturity of the men as compared with the women) from a position in the play in which they were bound to be criticised and mocked. Julia and Portia have their moments, but they are brief when set beside the opportunities given to Berowne and Bassanio. In *As You Like It*, however, the character with the greatest stage presence, with the most visible initiative, is a woman, Rosalind. This totally alters the bias of the play, the way it makes its pronouncements on courtship and love.

Rosalind is more mature, more poised, than love's spokesmen in the early comedies. She does not lay herself and what she speaks about open to ridicule, or at least gentle mockery, as Proteus, Berowne, Lysander and Demetrius did. Rosalind does what none of these other protagonists managed to do. She creates a context for the statements she makes about love which, because it is itself mocking and witty, neutralises the mockery and wit with which we, and the other characters, might otherwise be tempted to attack what it contains. Hence the ambiguities and uncertainties that were allowed to exist at the centre of our response to love in, say, *Love's Labour's Lost*, are here thrust to one side. The absurdity, the 'more-strange-than-true' aspect of romance, is absorbed into the poised acceptance of love that Rosalind makes; and so the maturity of Hippolyta and the French Princess is rendered less brittle. With the certainty about love that is guaranteed in Rosalind's person comes a new and comprehensive facility with wit, and an astringency that consorts well with the endorsement of sentiment at the heart of the play.

The wit is an expression of the poise given the three theoreticians of love – Rosalind, Touchstone, Jaques – to speak. Even Jaques' verse at II, vii has the colloquial dash-and-run of the prose, which is not altogether new in Shakespeare, though it is almost new to his comedies. Sly had used prose vigorously in *The Taming of the Shrew* and Launce had a good line in it in *The Two Gentlemen of Verona*. And, of course, there was Bottom in *A Midsummer Night's Dream*. But none of these could match the prose of Falstaff in *Henry IV* and, more to our purpose here, that of Benedick and Beatrice in *Much Ado about Nothing*. This is the most consummate example of a naturalised Euphuistic prose, preserving the balance and *exempla* of Lyly, but integrating them with informal speech patterns which give a vigour, a thrust to the repartee that Lyly could not have managed. Compare a couple of speeches from the two plays. This is Beatrice putting down her father's suggestions in the event of the Prince's wooing her at the ball:

If the Prince be too important, tell him there is measure in every thing, and so dance out the answer. For hear me, Hero: wooing, wedding, and repenting, is as a Scotch jig, a measure, and a cinquepace; the first suit is hot and hasty, like a Scotch jig, and full as fantastical; the wedding, mannerly modest as

a measure, full of state and ancientry; and then comes repent-
ance, and, with his bad legs, falls into the cinquepace faster
and faster, till he sink into his grave.

And this is Rosalind in her disguise as Ganymede, expatiating on
the power, or powerlessness, of love:

> The poor world is almost six thousand years old, and in all this
> time there was not any man died in his own person, videlicet,
> in a love-cause. Troilus had his brains dash'd out with a
> Grecian club; yet he did what he could to die before, and he is
> one of the patterns of love. Leander, he would have liv'd many
> a fair year though Hero had turn'd nun, if it had not been for
> a hot midsummer night; for, good youth, he went but forth to
> wash him in the Hellespont, and, being taken with the cramp,
> was drowned; and the foolish chroniclers of that age found it
> was – Hero of Sestos. But these are lies: men have died from
> time to time, and worms have eaten them, but not for love.

In both plays this prose is used as a corrective to the inflated
and vulnerable romantic verse which is spoken by the other
lovers – Claudio and Hero in *Much Ado*, Orlando, Silvius and
Phebe in *As You Like It*. But in *Much Ado* the two modes of
address rarely exist side by side, let alone interpenetrate. In their
big scenes Benedick and Beatrice keep themselves to themselves.
In this respect *As You Like It* is different. The mock wooing
of Rosalind/Ganymede by Orlando is at the centre of the play,
and Rosalind's scene with Phebe is one of the wittiest. Indeed,
As You Like It is constructed out of a series of contrasts between
different kinds of verbal strategies – those proper to verse and
those proper to prose. It is the culmination of a process that
began with Titania's wooing of Bottom, in *A Midsummer Night's
Dream*. Here prose and verse speeches exist side by side, and
when they move apart the prose, which for want of a better word
I shall say expresses a realistic assessment of the value of sentiment and other things as well, is spoken by male and female
parts, instead of by the clown, as it was in both *The Two Gentlemen of Verona* and *A Midsummer Night's Dream* (and later by
Launcelot Gobbo in *The Merchant of Venice*). By the time we
arrive at *As You Like It* the female lead has taken over the
'prose' role of the clown, and with it the critical temperament it

expresses. But she takes it over along with the active, initiative-
taking character we noticed in Julia and Portia (after Act IV).
Love and a realistic critique of love co-exist within a single person, at the centre of the play.

This explains my reference to Rosalind creating the context
within which she is to be appraised. It is a context made up
equally of the romantic idealism that is rendered absurd by
Orlando and Silvius and the different types of mockery and
criticism of romantic idealism that are represented by Touchstone
and Jaques. Rosalind creates it by taking over both alternatives
and subordinating them to her own requirements. By this means
they are got into proportion, the silliness contained in each in
their unmixed forms disappears in the world of mature and
'unillusioned' love she embodies. The witty prose she speaks
and thinks in allows Rosalind to see round both extremes and
to 'place' them within the circle of her own judgement.

We can see the way she does this in respect of Touchstone
and Jaques by looking at passages from two different scenes. The
first is from III, ii, where Touchstone, having heard Rosalind
read out one of the rhymes Orlando has written to her, replies
with a rhyme of his own and asks:

> *Touchstone*: This is the very false gallop of verses. Why do you
> infect yourself with them?
> *Rosalind*: Peace, you dull fool, I found them on a tree.
> *Touchstone*: Truly, the tree yields bad fruit.
> *Rosalind*: I'll graff it with you, and then I shall graff it with
> a medlar; then it will be the earliest fruit i'the' country: for
> you'll be rotten ere you be half ripe, and that's the right
> virtue of the medlar.
> *Touchstone*: You have said; but whether wisely or no, let the
> forest judge.

And the second is from IV, i, Rosalind's first (and only) meeting
with Jaques:

> *Jaques*: I have neither the scholar's melancholy, which is
> emulation; nor the musician's, which is fantastical; nor the
> courtier's, which is proud; nor the soldier's, which is ambitious;
> nor the lawyer's, which is politic; nor the lady's, which is nice;
> nor the lover's, which is all these: but it is a melancholy of

mine own, compounded of many simples, extracted from many objects, and indeed the sundry contemplation of my travels, in which my often rumination wraps me in a most humorous sadness.

Rosalind: A traveller! By my faith, you have great reason to be sad. I fear you have sold your own lands to see other men's; then, to have seen much and to have nothing is to have rich eyes and poor hands.

Jaques: Yes, I have gained my experience.

Enter Orlando.

Rosalind: And your experience makes you sad. I had rather have a fool to make me merry than experience to make me sad – and to travail for it too!

Orlando: Good day, and happiness, dear Rosalind!

Jaques: Nay then, God buy you, an you talk in blank verse.

Going.

Rosalind: (*as he goes*) Farewell, Monsieur Traveller. Look you lisp and wear strange suits; disable all the benefits of your own country; be out of love with your nativity, and almost chide God for making you that countenance you are; or I will scarce think you have swam in a gondola.

Rosalind does not attack Touchstone and Jaques head on. She corrects the criticism they make by attributing the nature of that criticism to distortions arising out of defects of character, and therefore of valuation, in each of their persons. She creates a firm basis for romantic love, not by providing any positive rationale – that is impossible – but by correcting the bias of its detractors. She exposes the limitations and distortions imposed on their powers of judgement by defects (mainly of self-knowledge) in their own characters.

That is one way she does it. Another is by her disguise as Ganymede, which enables her to give full expression to her love for Orlando whilst preserving a distancing effect, an obliquity, that removes any hint of the maudlin, the cloying, the overblown – the sort of thing that Gratiano and Nerissa were there to prevent in *The Merchant of Venice*. Shakespeare had tried out this device, with a less ambitious end in view, in his handling of Julia in *The Two Gentlemen of Verona*. Portia's disguise as the young lawyer was a variant of it too. It reaches its apogee in the business of Viola's disguise as Cesario in *Twelfth Night*. I want to defer my discussion of the boy–girl syndrome in Shakespeare until I come to that play. I shall limit my treatment of it here to the use it is put to in the Phebe–Silvius affair.

The contrast between the earnest contrivances of the lovers and the contrived banter of Rosalind brings out most of the advantages of the disguise. Romantic idealism has been transformed into a literary trick in Silvius's Arcadian speech, in spite of the sincerity of his love for Phebe which lies beneath the jumble of words he thinks he needs to express it. Or it is shrivelled up in Phebe's unimaginative and graceless common sense when she tells Silvius not to be a fool and stop supposing that anybody's eyes are capable of killing. Where to take your stand between fancy and sheer literalism, that is the problem. Rosalind's disguise shows her the way. In it she can combine superficial mockery and real passion, which Orlando may not be able to see, but we can (perhaps Celia can too). In iv, i, for example, it allows her both the ' "day" without the "ever" ' and the 'blind rascally boy' speeches. The last of these reminds us of Berowne's verse speech in iii, i of *Love's Labour's Lost*. It is not only the change of expressive forms that shows us how far we have travelled in the interim. Celia is more unimpressed than the Princess of France was. 'And I'll sleep' she replies to Rosalind's 'I'll go find a shadow and sigh till he come.' But the circumstances in which Rosalind says this, and the clothes in which she says it, convince us that there is more to what she says and feels than there ever was to Berowne.

Mark van Doren sums up Shakespeare's achievement with Rosalind very well. Her criticism of love and the pastoral life, he says, is unremitting, 'yet she has not annihilated them. Rather, she has preserved them by removing the flaws of their softness. . . . Romance has been tested in her until we know it cannot shatter; laughter had made it sure of itself. There is only one thing sillier than being in love, and that is thinking it is silly to be in love. Rosalind skips through both errors to wisdom.' Elegantly and succinctly put. Orlando, Silvius and William exemplify the first silliness. It is left to Touchstone and Jaques to exemplify the second. It is time now we took a look at the malcontent and the fool, to discover the different ways in which they do this.

Even in 1598 the figure of the malcontent would have been familiar to Elizabethans, although the two most celebrated theatrical representations of him – Hamlet and John Marston's Malevole (in a play called *The Malcontent*) had not been invented yet. He was the 'drop-out' of the 1590s and 1600s, the sophisticated young man who had probably been to Italy, read Machiavelli, read Castiglione's *Courtier* and probably been revolted by it, and come to the conclusion that the world was an unweeded garden that had grown to seed. He usually wore black and affected what would later be known as a Hamletian indifference to society. In other words, he was type-cast and his attitudes would have been recognisable at once as belonging to a contemporary fad. Of course they might go beyond it, as obviously Hamlet's did. But they need not – and it is noticeable that in his most melancholy moods, Jaques keeps the best company, switching from one dispossessed duke to another as the play proceeds.

The fool had a more complex role to play. He shared with the malcontent an acknowledged 'position' within the company or court. Indeed, his was at once more official and less clearly defined. One thing about the fool worth noticing is that he has no counterpart in earlier Shakespearean drama. After Touchstone in *As You Like It* he appears twice again, as Feste in *Twelfth Night*, and as the anonymous fool in *King Lear*. (There is also Lavache in *All's Well that Ends Well*.) None of the other comic characters had been or were to be professional fools, the types Leslie Hotson describes in *Shakespeare's Motley*. They were clowns – usually servants or constables by profession. Touchstone was a professional fool, like the real life fool we know best in the person of Henry VIII's jester, Tom Skelton. As such he would wear a long coat woven out of threads of different colours, and he would have a very privileged position within the household. In *King Lear* the fool receives harsh words and the odd buffet or two, but the King keeps him in his service and does not treat him as he does the loyal Kent, for example. He tells the King much more uncomfortable home truths than Kent ever does, and yet by using folly as a stalking horse he avoids the same fate. As Shakespeare moved from *As You Like It* to *Twelfth Night* to *King Lear* the character of the fool became ever more melancholy and wistful and truthful. Here Touchstone has some of the refinement of Feste, and all of his wit (in fact a great deal more). What he does not have is his piercing sadness. It is not that sort of play. We do not know who played Jaques in the Globe production. But we know that an actor new to the company, Robert Armin, played Touchstone, and was to play Feste and the fool in *King Lear* in subsequent productions. For the moment, neither his sadness nor his song have found a place in the play.

Both Touchstone and Jaques are exponents of a reductive humour, that is to say of a temperament that delights in stripping away the fantasies and deceits that are believed to clothe the body of truth. Since truth appears to be made of clothes, however, the exercise is usually disastrous when taken to its extreme – as it is in Swift, for example. So in *As You Like It* neither of them is allowed to go to the furthest extremes, though Jaques comes near to it on occasion. His account of the seven ages of man is deeply cynical. Touchstone has a more ambivalent attitude, quizzically sceptical of both illusion and disillusion. His conversation with Corin at III, ii, is typical of him:

> *Corin*: And how like you this shepherd's life, Master Touchstone?
> *Touchstone*: Truly, shepherd, in respect of itself, it is a good life; but in respect that it is a shepherd's life, it is naught. In respect that it is solitary, I like it very well; but in respect that it is private, it is a very vile life. Now in respect it is in the fields, it pleaseth me well; but in respect it is not in the court, it is tedious. As it is a spare life, look you, it fits my humour well; but as there is no more plenty in it, it goes much against my stomach.

His insistence on having it both ways is a linguistic reflection of the double landscape in which the dialogue takes place. The two ways of looking at nature are transposed into two ways of appraising a situation. Touchstone's ability to see things from two points of view simultaneously is like Rosalind's. The difference is that he cannot make the affirmation that locks them together somewhere half-way between.

In the speech the balanced antitheses and *exempla* of Euphuism are used with a critical intent. Van Doren sums up its object in a probing paradox. 'Touchstone is without illusion;' he says, 'so much so that he will not claim that he can do without it.' His 'fault' lies in the stance he takes up towards the world of love and sentiment. Even his romance with Audrey is something to be half involved with and half to be contemplated in the light of his dry, mocking intelligence. That intelligence remains dry. It doesn't combine with the sentiment it exercises itself upon. The two sides of his nature remain polarised, the one looking at the other across a void his own scepticism has created.

If Jaques is 'too fond of believing he is wise to be as wise as he sounds', Touchstone is too sure of the terms according to which he has met illusion half way to convince us (and himself, perhaps) that such terms are not part of a greater illusion still. Only Rosalind has got it right and passed by on the other side of the struggle between sentiment and scepticism. This is why she can act as a norm around which the lovers and the cynics conduct their disputations and play out their scenes. But we should be mistaken if we supposed that as such she occupies a fixed position, an Aristotelian point of balance. Shakespeare knew that the norm is never fixed. It moves in strange ellipses around a central point that never existed. It is a principle of vitality, as well as judgement.

9

Twelfth Night

At our feast we had a play called 'Twelve Night or What You Will', much like the Commedy of Errores, or Menechmi in Plautus, but most like and neere to that in Italian called Ingani. A good practice in it to make the Steward beleeve his Lady widdowe was in love with him, by counterfeyting a letter as from his Lady in general termes, telling him what she liked best in him, and prescribing his gesture in smiling, his apparaile, etc, and then when he came to practise making him beleeve they tooke him to be mad.

That was how Robert Manningham described a production of *Twelfth Night* at the Middle Temple at Candlemas (2 February) 1602. It was not the first performance, which must have taken place at least a year earlier, as Shakespeare wrote the play before or during 1600. But the record of it that Manningham gives (Manningham was a barrister at the Temple) provides us with two useful pieces of information. The play was suitable for private performance on one or other of the festive occasions at the Inns of Court and elsewhere during the winter (Leslie Hotson believes that the first performance was in honour of another festive occasion – the entertainment of Orsini, Duke of Bracciano at Whitehall on 6 January 1601). We do not have to take its title too seriously. None of the three 'contemporary' occasions when we know it was performed fell on a Twelfth Night. Two of them (this one and one in 1623 at court) fell on Candlemas. The other (for King James in 1618) on Easter Monday. Only Hotson's hypothetical first production took place on an actual Twelfth Night.

It would be pleasant to think that *Twelfth Night* was originally a part of the Twelfth Night revels because, in spite of the absence of dances in the play, its action does seem to be peculiarly

seasonal. No other comedy has so clear a contrast between the
romantic affairs of the principals and the feasting, drinking and
merrymaking of the sub-plot. In no other comedy, either, does
the sub-plot occupy quite so much space, not even the Shylock
plot in *The Merchant of Venice* (if that can be called a sub-plot),
which is in bulk relatively small. In fact it is inaccurate to call
the action involving Toby, Sir Andrew, Feste, Maria and
Malvolio a sub-plot. Shakespeare invented it himself and added
it to the story he had taken from an early sixteenth century
play. He allows it to run parallel with what would otherwise
have been the main story, joining up with it momentarily
during Cesario's duel with Sir Andrew. We can tell that it had
always attracted a fair amount of attention not merely by
looking at the list of famous actors who played the part of Sir
Toby and Sir Andrew in their time, but also by noting the fact
that the title of the play was given out as *Malvolio* in the 1623
production.

Shakespeare seems to have entered into the spirit of the
occasion by putting all his best ideas to work. *Twelfth Night* is
a collection of self-borrowings, standing at one end of Shakespeare's achievement in the genre of romantic comedy much
as *The Two Gentlemen of Verona* stood at the other. The early
play looked forward to everything that was to come; the later
one looks back to everything that has been. Viola disguised as
Cesario looks back to Julia disguised as a page by way of
Rosalind disguised as Ganymede. Antonio, Sebastian's melancholy friend, looks back to his namesake in *The Merchant of
Venice* by way of Jaques – though Jaques' cynicism and bitter-
ness have been lost in the process. Both Antonios are also deeply
loyal friends. Armin changes roles from Touchstone to Feste.
Slender is transformed into Aguecheek and Falstaff into Sir
Toby. The eavesdropping scene (*on* Malvolio *by* Maria and
the others) is taken from *Much Ado about Nothing*, which in
turn was taken from *Love's Labour's Lost*. There are permutations on almost every stock Shakespearean scene and variants of
many stock Shakespearean characters. In this respect, as in
others, *Twelfth Night* is the crown of Shakespeare's achievement
in romantic comedy.

All these are matters of detail. The outline of the plot as a
whole reminds us most of a play I have not included in this

list of local borrowings. Manningham was surely right when he said that *Twelfth Night* was 'much like the Commedy of Errores' because so much of the Viola plot turns upon the business of mistaken identities, with Cesario and Sebastian as the successors to the two Antipholuses. There is, however, the enormous difference, not just that there are no Dromios in *Twelfth Night*, but that for most of the time Viola's twin is not on-stage. The first time we see him is in III, iii, which means that the ensuing complications have less than half a play to work themselves out. In any case the twins are not really alike. How can they be when one is a boy and the other a girl? Only at the different level of illusion represented by the fact that both characters were actually played by boy actors – a separate matter I shall deal with a little later. What happens, then, is that the broad comedy issuing from the business of mistaken identities in *Comedy of Errors* is reserved for Sir Toby and the revellers in *Twelfth Night*, and *because* they are revellers it takes a different form and encourages the audience to take up a different attitude towards it. Then in Acts IV and V, with the arrival on the scene of Sebastian, the disappearance from it ('within') of Malvolio, and the degeneration of Toby and Aguecheek into a function of the Viola plot, the errors of *this* play take over, and, in my opinion, cause a distinct lowering of the play's temperature.

Manningham also mentioned that, though *Twelfth Night* reminded him of the *Menaechmi* (upon which, we remember, *Comedy of Errors* was based), it was 'most like and neere to that in Italian called Inganni', actually *GI' Ingannati*, which is, translated, *The Deceived*. Who is deceived in our play? We might answer, who is not? Whether we look in the plot that Shakespeare took (indirectly) from the Italian, or in the plot he made up to put beside it, we shall discover deceit piled on deceit. Olivia and Orsino are both deceived by Cesario. Antonio is deceived into believing that Sebastian is dead (though he seems to have faith in the fact that he is not). Olivia is deceived into believing she is marrying Cesario, when in fact she is marrying Sebastian. In the 'Malvolio' plot, Malvolio himself is deceived by Maria and the others in the orchard and by Feste pretending to be Sir Topas in the dark house. Sir Andrew and Sir Toby are deceived into thinking Sebastian is Cesario who is in fact

Viola. Sir Andrew is deceived into supposing Cesario is a fine swordsman and Cesario is deceived into supposing Sir Andrew is the same. The play is a tissue of deceits and misunderstandings – misunderstandings that have been caused by deceit *and* the workings of chance, in the form of the outcome of the shipwreck. The action of *Twelfth Night* is a veritable Comedy of Errors.

But it is not really like *The Comedy of Errors*. The combination of misunderstandings and surprises, which incorporates so many of the devices tried and perfected in the comedies Shakespeare had already written, does not result in the creation of a plot. What in one kind of play would have produced an intrigue, here produces a masquerade. The one tends in the direction of farce, the other in the direction of romance and festive celebration. We have already noticed that until Act iv Shakespeare makes little use of his 'deceptions' in the way of forging links between them that would produce narrative tension and draw the audience's attention towards the working out of the plot. When he does do this, from Act iv onwards, the result is not disaster, but it is, I think, disappointment. The more important the plot, the less interesting the play.

The precipitation of Cesario into the affairs of the two households is the occasion for a sequence of scenes strung loosely along the line of the romance narrative. How loosely emerges only after a careful rereading of, say, the scenes that contain Cesario's 'interviews' with Orsino and Olivia. Otherwise the outcrop of the intrigue towards the end can leave a false impression. Here (in Act i, iv–v, Act ii, iv, Act iii, i and Act iii, iv) each little sequence composes itself into a speaking picture, a dramatic cameo. It does contribute something to the plot. But it is not for this reason that we enjoy it. Also, the scenes with Maria, Sir Toby and Sir Andrew before Act iv have little or no connection with the transactions going on between Orsino and Olivia. The only link is through Sir Andrew's rivalry with Cesario for Olivia's hand, and that is hardly developed in the first three acts. These scenes exist in isolation from the events that are going on around them. The connection between them is more atmospheric than narrative, a matter of the 'clowns' being incorporated within the setting of Olivia's house and garden and, in being so, making it the more vivid and substantial. After all, without them it would be both a miserable and an inactive place. Their songs and banter are required to set off both the melancholy of Olivia and the pomposity of Malvolio.

The scenes in Olivia's house and garden hang together more by virtue of their contribution to the sense of 'decorum' – decorum maintained or disrupted – than to the plot. 'Decorum' is intimately associated with the atmospheric settings of the play, the kind of thing Professor Barber is referring to in this extract from his book:

> Throughout the play a contrast is maintained between the taut, restless, elegant court, where people speak a nervous verse, and the free-wheeling household of Olivia, where, except for the intense moments of Olivia's amorous interviews with Cesario, people live in an easygoing prose. The contrast is another version of pastoral. The household is more than any one person in it. People keep interrupting each other, changing their minds, letting their talk run out into foolishness – and through it all Shakespeare expresses the day-by-day going on of a shared life.

'The household is more than any one person in it.' How many nineteenth-century novelists have tried to give the same impression – with very different methods of course, proper to the different form of fiction in which they were working. That is what I mean by decorum – everything fitting in, nothing being out of place; a sense of shared life at different levels of authority, status, personality and relationship. The time also produces variations in the positions characters believe they fit into. Time of day, and time of year. When the play opens, the time of year has a particular importance.

It is Twelfth Night, a time when you do what you will and 'quite athwart goes all decorum'. It is permissible to take every opportunity to produce a temporary comic disturbance in the normal goings-on of the household. True, Olivia is scarcely in the mood to put up with this, and so Malvolio is in possession of an excellent weapon with which to ensure that decorum is preserved – quite indecorously on Twelfth Night. But Sir Toby and Maria will not be put off. They play their part in producing deceptions which fulfil the requirements of the season and extend

far beyond the confines of their own plot. For the disturbances
here take two forms, both of which involve some kind of deception. Superficially, there are the plot deceptions revolving around
the disguised figure of Viola/Cesario, and later involving her
twin brother – and there is the gulling of Malvolio in a Twelfth
Night prank. There is also the more basic *self*-deception of both
Orsino and Olivia, and the disturbance that the disguised Viola
undergoes as a result of her newly awakened love for Orsino.
Shakespeare uses the superficial disturbances not as ends in themselves (as he had done in *The Comedy of Errors*) but as means
to an end: the end of portraying and resolving basic disturbances
which lie far beneath them, but which connect with them at
several sensitive points and are in turn made use of by them –
as instruments – to 'bring themselves to rights' at the close. The
'plot'-deceptions act as metaphors to express the emotional misunderstandings and surprises that constitute the real subject of
the play.

As a result, the plot is less watertight than it was in *The
Comedy of Errors*. There are a number of typical romance
non-sequiturs, the psychological narrative equivalents of Bo-
hemia's coastline in *The Winter's Tale*. For example Viola
is not given satisfactory reasons for pretending that she doesn't
recognise Antonio as her brother Sebastian's man at v, i. Her
supposition that Sebastian must still be alive was confirmed at
the end of III, iv, when Antonio, on his first appearance in Illyria,
mentioned him by name. As far as I can see she has nothing
to gain by putting Antonio to any further discomfort. Shakespeare is fumbling with the details of the twin brother/sister
plot because his interest in it is very much less than it is in the
romance of Olivia = Cesario/Viola = Orsino = Olivia. Even in a
farce, the superimposition of a disguise plot on a twins plot
would be asking a lot. And here Shakespeare isn't interested in
farce. So he chooses his priority, which is the disguise plot (where
he can develop his interest in romantic love), and waves goodbye
to the twins. But the plot as a whole has to be resolved, and so
Sebastian has to be brought on – not only to please Viola, but
to produce a suitable marriage partner for Olivia. This plays
havoc with the last act, in which so much has still to be resolved,
even though some of the material has been got out of the way
in the fourth. The play of mood and reflection which had been

so attractively presented in I–III has to disappear for much of
the time, returning only in one or two speeches by Sebastian
and Feste's song at the end. For the rest, the deceptions practised
by most of the characters in one way or another are all part of
the Twelfth Night confusions. They are a sort of multiple masquerade that eventually brings all to rights, resolving not merely
(in some ways not all) the mechanical confusions of identity,
and therefore of plot, but, more important, the inner self-
deceptions and immaturities that exist beneath the surface
deceptions.

All is brought to rights at the end of a play in which, in spite
of the fancifulness of the events, a great deal more resistance has
been set up than has been usual so far. True, there were times
in *The Merchant of Venice* when things looked black for Antonio.
But that was because of an evil force entering the world of the
Venetians from outside. Shylock was an alien growth, an external
threat; whereas Malvolio, his nearest equivalent in *Twelfth
Night*, is the steward of Olivia's household, a man with certain
rights and duties, of which he is very conscious. He is a square
peg in a round hole, but Shylock wasn't a peg at all – he didn't
fit into anything, not even uncomfortably. In any case Malvolio
scarcely constitutes a threat. If he does, he does so only in respect
of the festivities – not the love affairs which take place within
them. So we can say that in *Twelfth Night* there is very little
disturbance caused by conflict in the plot. There is no Egeus,
Don John, Shylock – not even an Oliver or a Duke Frederick,
to create a danger or impose a threat. Even so, we are disturbed,
and not simply as a result of the complications (hardly the
conflict) set up by the disguises and the mistakings. In spite of the
Twelfth Night revelry, in spite of Sir Toby's drinking and Maria's
wit, there is a strain of sadness, of complaint running through
this play that makes it a very different experience from *As You
Like It*. It comes of a disturbance characters feel within themselves that is not attributable to the plot at all, but to the very
nature of what, and how, they feel.

Take the very first words of the play. They are spoken by
Orsino to Curio and his other attendants before we have had
the opportunity of hearing about his apparently hopeless love
for Olivia. Their subject is, of course, love; but love of a kind
we have heard little of before in Shakespeare:

If music be the food of love, play on,
Give me excess of it, that, surfeiting,
The appetite may sicken, and so die.
That strain again! It had a dying fall.
O, it came o'er my ear like the sweet sound
That breathes upon a bank of violets,
Stealing and giving odour. Enough, no more;
'Tis not so sweet now as it was before.
O spirit of love, how quick and fresh art thou!
That, notwithstanding thy capacity
Receiveth as the sea, nought enters there,
Of what validity and pitch soe'er,
But falls into abatement and low price
Even in a minute. So full of shapes is fancy,
That it alone is high fantastical.

The first eight lines tell us nothing new. What Orsino has to say
about music is beautifully affected, eloquently self-indulgent –
a fact that has been proved in countless elocution classes. But
with the address to the spirit of love that follows, things take on
a very different complexion. It is not just that Orsino's behaviour
as a lover is quite different from that of earlier more active
suitors like Berowne and Helena, both of whom believed that
love has the totally opposite effect to the one Orsino says it has
here – of adding vigour rather than taking it away. Orsino is,
after all, another malcontent figure, and is therefore welcome to
the privilege of deceiving himself in this way. What I want to
draw attention to is the way the language Shakespeare uses to
describe his hero's spiritual lassitude changes in the last seven
lines of the speech, the first speech in the play, and by virtue of
that fact one that is going to affect considerably how we respond
to the events that follow.

The change is signalled by the rhyme that closes the first half
of the speech. After that, the pulse of the verse quickens, and
the combination of abstract and concrete nouns – 'capacity',
'validity', 'pitch', 'abatement', 'price' – that is characteristic
of mature Shakespearean blank verse takes over from the elegant
patterning and conventional imagery of the more lyrical opening.
The language has become exploratory instead of eloquent, it
embodies rather than describes feeling. There was already a hint

of this in the second and third lines, with their emphasis on appetite and disease. Here the dominating image is that of the sea. Eating, disease, the sea – images relating to these take us forward to *Hamlet* and *Troilus and Cressida*, and back to the sonnets (in I, v Cesario advises Olivia to marry Orsino so as to 'leave the world a copy of herself' – precisely Shakespeare's own advice to the fair friend of the sonnets). They also take us forward into *Twelfth Night* itself. Imagery of this kind crops up throughout the play; corruption, appetite, the sea all recurring in the important speech Cesario makes to Orsino at II, iv:

> *Orsino*: There is no woman's sides
> Can bide the beating of so strong a passion
> As love doth give my heart; no woman's heart
> So big to hold so much; they lack retention.
> Alas, their love may be call'd appetite –
> No motion of the liver, but the palate –
> That suffer surfeit, cloyment, and revolt;
> But mine is all as hungry as the sea,
> And can digest as much. Make no compare
> Between that love a woman can bear me
> And that I owe Olivia.
> *Viola*:   Ay, but I know –
> *Orsino*: What dost thou know?
> *Viola*: Too well what love women to men may owe.
> In faith, they are as true of heart as we.
> My father had a daughter lov'd a man,
> As it might be perhaps, were I a women,
> I should your lordship.
> *Orsino*:   And what's her history?
> *Viola*: A blank, my lord. She never told her love,
> But let concealment, like a worm i' the bud,
> Feed on her damask cheek. She pin'd in thought;
> And with a green and yellow melancholy
> She sat like Patience on a monument,
> Smiling at grief. Was not this love indeed?
> We men may say more, swear more, but indeed
> Our shows are more than will; for still we prove
> Much in our vows, but little in our love.

What a wonderful scene this is – one of the 'cameos' I referred to above. But it is not just wonderful. The lovers' ambitions extend as far as they are to do in *Troilus and Cressida* two years later but, as in that play, it really looks as if 'the act's a slave to limit' and the execution of what the will and the spirit propose is hopelessly confined. The limitlessness of Orsino's passion is pictured as being like the sea. But when the sea is hungry, it eats into the shore, destroys what is not itself. Orsino's hunger feeds on itself. Similarly Viola's concealment of love eats at the flesh that conceals it, corrupts the body that is so much more akin to it than the bud ever is to the worm. The sonnets are full of the devouring sea, and cankers stud the text of both the sonnets (e.g. xxxv) and slightly later plays like *Hamlet* (Hamlet's observations on his mother's marriage to Claudius are full of images of corruption). Olivia may be a different case. She is a more typical example of the disdainful lady, in spite of the reality of the dead brother in the background. But Orsino is certainly not just another silly young man with self-indulgent ideas about love and courtship. His melancholy has some substance. It is a part of reality as well as of the deceptions we practise on reality.

We can verify this by reading or, better, watching the whole scene (II, iv) being played. For in it Orsino is not as single-mindedly bemoaning the fruitlessness of his love for Olivia as is sometimes supposed. His feeling has Cesario as much as Olivia as its object though, of course, Olivia is its ostensible object – that is to say, Orsino *thinks* that Olivia is its object. But by this time Viola/Cesario has made herself a place at Orsino's court; and a familiarity is developing between 'page' and master which Viola recognises as romantic love but which Orsino is still too infatuated with Olivia to understand. If this is so, Orsino's lines about the destructiveness of his passion cannot be explained away by pointing to the false centre from which both they and the 'love' they express spring. Nor do they take upon themselves this character as a result of the confusion of aims and objects they betray. The dissatisfaction the Duke gives voice to is rooted in the nature of love, not only in the artificial make-believe romance he felt, or thought he felt, for Olivia; and it is not to be attributed to the uncertainty, absurdity, brevity of love ('too like the lightning'), as it was in the earlier affairs. Love itself is unsatisfactory, a power that absorbs energy and aspiration rather than one that gives them a new impetus, 'adding a precious seeing to the eye' and so on. Cesario's reply corroborates this view of love, with its history of the concealed 'Viola' who 'died' of love, 'Smiling at grief'. And this history in its turn draws our attention to a feature of the play which is vital to our proper response to the whole, namely the matter of Viola's identity in these middle scenes.

At first glance it may seem that there is no need to make a fuss about this. In Shakespeare, girls are always disguising themselves as boys. They have done so in the past, and they will do so again (in *Cymbeline*). In *As You Like It*, the play that immediately preceded this one, Rosalind dressed up as Ganymede and 'wooed' Orlando in disguise. The difference lies in the way this wooing is presented. For in *As You Like It* Ganymede doesn't exist. In *Twelfth Night* Cesario does – as a real presence to the audience. When we look at Ganymede we pass right through her to Rosalind, who is merely using him as a device. Rosalind is always before our eyes, a millimetre beneath the paint and clothes that are all that really exist of Ganymede. She is a poised, adept intelligence making use of a mask. Orlando couldn't, and didn't fall in love with a mask, even though the silly Phebe could. In *Twelfth Night*, on the contrary, it isn't just the silly Phebe sort of person who falls in love with Cesario. In any case, there is a lot of difference between Phebe and Olivia, affected though they both are. Also the Orlando figure, here Orsino, is clearly falling more and more in love with him, even though he can't see the change in direction which his love is taking. He is too interested in 'love' to be much aware of its real object. We have already looked at the 'My father had a daughter' scene at II, iv. By the time we have got to v, i, Orsino's jealousy of Cesario and Olivia has grown to something approaching Othelloan proportions:

Why should I not, had I the heart to do it,
Like to the Egyptian thief at point of death,
Kill what I love? – a savage jealousy
That sometimes savours nobly.

He is talking about Cesario, not Olivia. His exaggerated response to Cesario's favour with his lady is ambivalent. The presence on the stage of both 'partners' during the tirade brings out very delicately the ambiguity of Orsino's shift in feeling. He fails to distinguish the object of his anger from the object of his love.

The more other characters feel towards a single character, the more that character's reality comes home to us – even if common sense tells us that it is only a façade. First Olivia, then Orsino, fall in love with Cesario and become subject to fits of jealousy in consequence. Cesario, for his part, has to convey Orsino's love-speeches to Olivia. Viola has to express her own love for Orsino in the guise of Cesario, talking about his sister and an unnamed suitor. The result of this is that not merely Cesario, but everything about him – his past, for instance – acquires a phantom life, a life we know is not real but which haunts the play nevertheless, getting into the interstices of its plotting and acting as a 'ghosting' around the picture that we acually see. So, the dead sister comes to a dramatic life, a tragic story lying behind the comic, romantic story that occupies the forefront of the stage. We 'know' that the sister is 'really' Viola herself, trying to get out, in make-believe, from her restrictive disguise as Cesario. At the same time we apprehend her story as an event which fades into the background of the play, making its contribution to the sadness and plaintiveness that are felt everywhere. In doing so it joins with other 'events' in what I will call the 'shadow play', the tragedy that 'ghosts' the romance – with the betrayal of Antonio by Sebastian, and the dismissal of Feste.

The part of Feste was tailor-made for Robert Armin who, you will remember, had replaced Will Kempe as the main funny man of the Lord Chamberlain's Company in 1599. Perhaps 'funny man' is the wrong word to describe him. Unfortunately we have no description of any of his performances that would tell us how he behaved on the stage. But his fooling was evidently delicate, wistful and refined; and he could sing. In *Twelfth Night* he has four songs, all but one of which are on the theme of death and disappointment. One of them, 'Come away, come away, death' is placed right in the middle of Orsino's talk with Cesario that we have just passed over.

> Not a flower, not a flower sweet,
>   On my black coffin let there be strewn;
> Not a friend, not a friend greet
>   My poor corpse where my bones shall be thrown;

It provides a mournful backcloth to Cesario's history of his sister's death. Throughout the play this background of melancholy song reinforces the images of corruption and of the sea – together threatening the romances of the lovers with their dark shadow and hints of impending disaster.

Viola's story; the recent deaths of Olivia's father and brother; Orsino's inexplicable dissatisfaction; the recurring imagery of the all-swallowing sea, corrupted forms of life disintegrating and declining; Feste's songs; minor, oblique references to such things as 'The spinsters and the knitters in the sun,/And the free maids that weave their thread with bones' who used to sing the 'old song' Feste sings now: the combined effect of all these is to create an impression of the passage of time and the reality of mortality which has not been present in any of the other comedies (We noticed it also in *Henry IV*, especially *Part 2*.). In Act v of *As You Like It*, the page's song on 'spring time' comfortably incorporates the line 'How that life was but a flower' into its easy gaiety and delight in the season. After all, flowers return with each spring, though they die in winter. At the close of *Twelfth Night* Feste's song gives no such comfort. Earlier in the play time was, and in a sense remains, an agency by which, in Viola's words, all will be brought to rights – 'O time, thou must untangle this, not I'. It became something to be joked away by Sir Toby, to Malvolio – 'We did keep time, sir, in our catches.' But finally, time has become something different and less manageable: more than a process in which 'nature to her bias' draws the confused but ultimately lucky loves of the characters; and more than something to be used as the subject of a joke and 'kept' in a song – perhaps the only way of keeping it. Feste's song gathers to itself all the unhappiness that was submerged in the other songs, in the imagery, in the 'ghosting', and in the comic treatment of Malvolio's last words – on revenge: all the things, in fact, that the foolings of Sir Toby and Maria kept at bay. In the song the thread of melancholy that turned and twisted about these incidents comes into its own. It is black, and unbreakable.

In *As You Like It* Jaques' speech on the seven ages of man (II, vii) was easily contained in the total action of the scenes in Arden. Jaques was a comic butt. He thought he was the satirist, but in fact he was the object of a mockery that passed beyond the need for satire. Rosalind's poise and certainty took note of his 'discoveries' and made them a part of her own point of view – put them in their proper place. Feste is not a comic butt. He is not, in the end, the object of satire or criticism of any kind. He is the spokesman for all that lay un*said* in the narrative of *Twelfth Night*, and it is not easy, perhaps not possible, for the play to know how to 'place' his discoveries about time, death, the sheer difficulty of living. The brittleness of Jaques' insights into the human condition (as also the more flexible accommodations of Touchstone) is replaced by a futile and wistful resignation – 'But that's all one and our play is done.'

After all, Feste has been three times lucky. 'Now you see, sir, how your fooling grows old.' That was Malvolio. You would expect that sort of dismissive treatment from him. But Maria had said much the same thing not long before, and she doesn't lack sympathy with the fool. Maybe next time he will be thrust outside Olivia's garden, out into the wind and the rain that whistle through the refrain of his song. There is a world where nature draws nothing to her bias, or does so at great cost and with enormous personal damage. For Feste, 'What's to come is still unsure.' *Twelfth Night* is a comedy. When the play is done and the song is sung, Feste will retire through one of the stage exits into the warmth and companionship of Olivia's household. For Shakespeare, however, what was to come was growing surer and surer. True, the note of perplexity sounds for a year or so. Then we emerge into the world beyond the court and beyond the household. It is cold, bare, and tragic. There are few songs, only snatches. And the fool is hanged.

Measure for Measure

Shakespeare never wrote like Ben Jonson, but he came close to it in *Measure for Measure*. Not in the detail, though some of the Duke's distasteful practical jokes remind us of the jokes Jonson's characters play on one another. The *spirit* of the thing is Jonsonian – Jonson without the frenzy and *with* saving graces, the literal sense of which I shall try to explain.

In *The Art of the Drama* Eric Bentley distinguishes between two kinds of comedy. In one there is a contrast between 'a frivolous manner and a grim meaning. The tone says: life is fun. The undertone suggests that life is a catastrophe.' The extreme example of this is comedy 'in which the final curtain has to fall to save us from a veritable cataclysm'. I think you will agree that this is often the case in Jonson. There is another kind of comedy, however, which works on a totally different principle. In it, romantic misadventures occur on a grand scale and yet 'a happy ending is somehow implicit from the beginning. ... A surface of the "terrible" conceals beneath it a kind of cosmic beneficence, a metaphysically guaranteed good luck.' This is usually Shakespeare's practice: 'for grim statements in a gay style are substituted benign statements in a style not without solemnity.' True of *A Midsummer Night's Dream* and *The Merchant of Venice*? I think so. Of *As You Like It*? Certainly. Of *Twelfth Night*? Well, yes, but. ... Basically it is true for Shakespeare, typical of his manner at its best. We find it again – shaped rather differently, but in outline the same – in the late comedies. Between *Twelfth Night* and *Cymbeline*, though, we pass through a group of plays that are not like the ones Bentley describes. But then, neither are they like the first kind. As I said, Shakespeare never wrote like Jonson. *All's Well that Ends Well*, *Troilus and Cressida*, and *Measure for Measure* are neither one thing nor the other. Some critics are not even sure they are comedies.

Measure for Measure is a comedy. But what kind of comedy?

It ends with the 'benign statements in a style not without solemnity' characteristic of the second type. To many of us, however, they seem oddly out of place. We have difficulty in conceiving of the betrothal of Isabella and the Duke in the same terms as we do the betrothals of Benedick and Beatrice, Orlando and Rosalind, Orsino and Viola. It is a 'satisfactory' ending, and in that sense it is 'happy'. But, as I said of *Twelth Night*, there are reservations, reservations which I think we must take even more seriously in this later play. Why is this? For one thing, because nobody brought a human head on stage in *Twelfth Night*. For another, we didn't follow Malvolio into the dark house, the prison. And for another, there were no rats, no brothels, no sciatica in Illyria. These are mere details. They remind us of the atmosphere in which the comic business of the play is enacted. Bawds, prisons, the hangman's rope and the head of a dead pirate – the conspicuous props of *Measure for Measure*. It takes more than a solemn, and rather tedious, last act to take the taste of them out of our mouths. Yet *Measure for Measure* shares with other comedies of Shakespeare one thing that few critics feel called upon to discuss. It is funny. Unpleasant, unsavoury, uninspiring – but funny. We have to ask ourselves why this is.

Measure for Measure was written at least three years after *Twelfth Night*. It probably followed *Hamlet*, *Othello* and *Troilus and Cressida*. This chronological proximity to the middle tragedies has confirmed the play's critics in their view that it was conceived in a different spirit from the early and mature romantic comedies. It shares this spirit with *Hamlet*, *Troilus* and *All's Well*. In each of these plays we can identify at least two basic differences from everything that has gone before, certainly from every comedy that has gone before. Shakespeare's interest in the springs of conduct, in what makes men act as they do, has developed beyond the stage it has reached in slightly earlier plays – *Henry IV* and *Julius Caesar* – in which that interest was strong. More deliberately than anywhere else in his work, Shakespeare has conducted his inquiry into human behaviour in a spirit of extremism. On the one hand is human motive fed by passions that are mysterious, complex and powerful: on the other, the abstract ethical concepts according to which men either think they act or desperately try to act – honour, justice, value.

Then, when tensions have been set up as a result of discrepancies that emerge between what men *would* do and what they *can* do, Shakespeare sets to work to undermine the usefulness, even the validity, of the concepts and principles in question. As they disintegrate under the pressure of the writer's scepticism and the characters' behaviour, the action becomes more and more confused, and more and more wayward, directionless. The comic endings of *Measure for Measure* and *All's Well* are substitutes for Bentley's final curtain that falls to save us all from a veritable cataclysm. *Hamlet* ends with a cataclysm. *Troilus* ends in a mess. *Troilus* is probably the most realistic and consistent of the plays in this respect.

Compare the way the idea of 'the pastoral life' is developed in *As You Like It* with the way any of the ideas in these plays is developed. The meaning of 'pastoral' is clarified in a number of conversation-pieces. It remains an idea, something separate from the people who talk about it – a subject for disputation (and song). It helps to reveal errors of attitude and flaws of disposition. But it does this by letting us see the way different characters handle the idea of pastoral life, not by engaging our interest in the way the idea works its way through their experience and is transformed and perverted in individual cases. We know what is meant by the pastoral life; and we know what attitudes to life and love are conventionally held to be parts of its substance. All that matters, then, is the position each character takes up in relation to it, a position which is presented intellectually. Our minds delight to play over it, we are amused by the wit that expresses it. But we are not called upon to respond to the tension characters feel between holding fast to an idea and accepting responsibility for their conduct, as we do so often in these later plays.

The meaning of 'pastoral' is clear, and so are the attitudes all the characters of *As You Like It* take towards it. We do not know with the same certainty what is meant by the abstract concept, value, that lies at the centre of *Troilus and Cressida*, because the characters there lose sight of the principle at issue as they try to make their behaviour consonant with their understanding of it. In the Trojan Council (II, ii) Priam, Hector, Troilus, Paris and Helenus are not even agreed as to its ideal or real existence. Their arguments do not spring from a common agreement as to what they are arguing about. A practical matter – whether or not Helen should be handed over to the Greeks – is rapidly converted into a highly abstruse philosophical debate on a subject no one of them defines in the same way as another. Their attitudes towards a single idea are so much a part of their characters, so rooted in their individuality, that the idea itself is in danger of disintegration. The closer character and idea move towards each other, the more the idea ceases to be practically useful or intellectually viable. It becomes simply the intellectual token of a distinct personality and is in its individual interpretations subject to change with the change in fortunes of the character who holds fast to it. Troilus feels differently about 'value' after he has lost Cressida from the way he felt before he did so.

The same with the idea of justice in *Measure for Measure*. The issue is similar to the one successfully evaded in Act IV of *The Merchant of Venice* (by a legal quibble and the subordinate position of the scene) – namely, the relationship between secular justice and the idea of divine mercy in a Christian state. The way the issue is handled is similar to the way the complementary issue is handled in *Troilus and Cressida*. By the end of the play, we are even less sure than the characters are of what we mean by justice and mercy and the capacity of human beings to give and receive them.

The difference between the status of ideas in the early comedies and here leads to large-scale formal readjustments. Conversation and debate give place to dramatic clash and confrontation. Both the characters and the situations in which they find themselves exert pressure on the principle which the principle cannot, or looks as if it cannot, withstand. In fact they create the terms for the definition of the principle, but do not go the necesssary and comforting step further – of setting guidelines for the arrangement of the terms. What in *As You Like It* was manipulated to set off, to throw into relief, aspects of character and temperament, in *Measure for Measure* is worked through from the inside, becomes a part of the springs of conduct which make character what it is. What in *As You Like It* was at the same time a technique for illuminating character and an object of amused contemplation and 'play', becomes in *Measure for Measure* a determinant of character. The abstract principle has become rooted in the minds and feelings of diverse characters. Subsequently it has grown into many different shapes, often fanciful, distorted and obscured by passion and interest. As a result it has lost the clear outline and stability that made it so useful a guide to conduct before; and is in turn made over into the object of a sceptical, but passionate, dramatic investigation.

Another peculiarity of these plays is Shakespeare's treatment of the sources. He had always been cavalier about this, dragging into a single play oddly contrasting materials from a number of different genres. Consequently in *Troilus and Cressida* we are not surprised to find him making use of comic–satiric material from Chaucer's poem on the subject and of heroic narrative from George Chapman's translation of the *Iliad*. What is surprising is that he appears to make no attempt to get them to work together harmoniously, to reduce the harsh contrasts between cynicism, romance and idealism that we find in the play. *Measure for Measure* presents a different problem. Here the oddity lies in the nature of the changes Shakespeare made to a single source, George Whetstone's translation in dramatic (1578) and narrative (1582) form of a story in Giraldi Cinthio's *Hundred Tales*. Shakespeare does two strange things. He strengthens Isabella's resistance to Angelo's advances to a point at which she becomes an undramatic, because unchangeable, character. And he increases the part played by the Duke in such a way as to take the responsibility of making the play interesting out of Isabella's hands when they have become too rigid to bear it any longer. The trouble is that Isabella wasn't the only person involved in her little plot. Angelo was the prime mover of it, and he remains very interesting indeed. But he is cut off, along with Isabella, to make way for the Duke and his plans. Clearly, Isabella and the Duke between them hold the key to Shakespeare's intentions. Let us look at them in turn.

In a play that is full of moral problems, Isabella raises more of them than anyone else. Should she give way to Angelo and save her brother, or should she refuse him and have her brother die? Should she agree to the bed trick, allowing Mariana to take her place with Angelo, or should she be consistent in her refusal to have anything to do with vice and deception? Should she approve in another what she cannot approve in herself? Most of us would agree with Dr Johnson's comment on Isabella's behaviour to

Claudio in the prison (III, i) that 'in Isabella's declaration there is something harsh, and something forced and far-fetched.' Would we not be justified in going further and saying that there is something forced and far-fetched about her conduct throughout? Before we go on to answer this we should bear in mind two things. First, Shakespeare's decision that she shall behave as she is represented as behaving in III, i and elsewhere was deliberate – he changed her more pliable disposition in the source. And her single-minded devotion to what she believes to be right (the principle of chastity) is similar to that of other loyal and single-minded heroines in the past – Julia, Helena (in *A Midsummer Night's Dream*), Rosalind – and in the future – Helena (in *All's Well that Ends Well*), Desdemona, Imogen. The difference is not in the temperament of the girl, but in the object on which it is fixed. In *Measure for Measure* that object is not a person, but a principle – an abstract idea of what is right. Shakespeare's treatment of Isabella is calculated, and consistent in all but this one important respect with his practice on previous occasions. By having her devote herself to a principle, he contrives to make that devotion unsympathetic, rigid, even ridiculous. This is the key to our response to Isabella. The main point about her is neither her frigidity nor her inhumanity, but her ridiculousness. Productions of the play often make the mistake of involving us too intimately in the dilemma she has to face and in the frame of mind in which she faces it. Also, of course, in involving us too intimately with Claudio, her brother – though here I think Shakespeare gives us more excuse. Once we see how ridiculous Isabella is we have a clue to how to approach the rest of the play. The fact that she is ridiculous has been too often obscured by the emphasis that has been placed on the moral element in the play. It *is* a play that makes us alive to the complexity of moral judgement. But it is more than that. It should not be made over into Shavian dialectic on the subject of sex and selfishness.

Let us take the scene singled out by Johnson in his notes to the play (III, i). The Duke has visited Claudio in prison and given him good advice – good on the assumption that Claudio believes he is to die. Be absolute for death. You lose little by it, for what have you to look forward to in life but fear, misery, work and disease? Only sleep, which is death's image, and is desired rather than shunned. His advice works. Claudio answers that:

To sue to live, I find I seek to die;
And, seeking death, find life. Let it come on.

A convenient frame of mind in which to face the executioner's
axe. But what happen's next? The Duke and the Provost leave
the stage as Isabella rushes in. Her behaviour is as tactless as
anything in the annals of English drama. 'Now, sister, what's the
comfort?' Claudio asks. Isabella proceeds to raise his hopes
with a heavy-handed irony that allows her to pronounce first of
all that his hopes are 'most good, most good indeed', and then
the hint at remedies and mercies she has no intention of making
available. Claudio manages to get in a few short questions between her raving histrionics, but he is finally forced to demand:
'Let me know the point.' She doesn't tell him it until she has
demonstrated how like a beetle he is, thus forcing from him a few
lines of heroic self-approval (later handed on to Cleopatra) to
cheer himself up. Now she can tell him what has transpired, first
of all trapping him in an embarrassed effort to bluff it out (after
all, he can't go back immediately on all that stuff about encoun-
tering darkness as a bride) and then, when the hard truth finally
dawns on him – he's going where Hamlet had refused to go a
couple of years before – pouring insult and vituperation on him.
'O you beast!' He is a 'faithless coward' and a 'dishonest wretch'
who must 'die quickly' after his sister has prayed a thousand
prayers for his death. Not the best way to see one's brother
off on the scaffold, I should have thought. But of a piece with
Isabella's character from the beginning.

Where did we first meet her? She was discovered in a convent
with Francisca, a nun, and her first words were a question about
how restricted her life there would be. 'And have you nuns no
further privileges?' she had asked, to which Francisca, getting
hold of the wrong end of the stick, had replied: 'Are not these
large enough?' Why do you want to be a nun if you are looking
for privileges? But that was where she was wrong. Isabella had
hoped for less, not more, privileges:

I speak not as desiring more,
But rather wishing a more strict restraint
Upon the sisterhood, the votaries of Saint Clare.

When Lucio arrives immediately after this little speech, he con-
firms the impression of Isabella we have already acquired. His

cheeky innuendoes about her virginity quickly disappear when he realises who she is and remembers what he wants to get out of her. He will not jest and seem the lapwing as he does with other young women. He holds her 'as a thing enskied and sainted', an 'immortal spirit' to be talked with 'as with a saint'. Thus pacified and drawn down from the full height from which she is doubtless peering at Lucio, she manages the pregnantly ambiguous line 'You do blaspheme the good in mocking me', leaving it for us to decide whether she *is* the good or whether she is so infinitely beneath it that for Lucio to pretend she is it represents a heinous sin. So her behaviour is exaggerated from the first. Her movement between extremes of self-approval and self-abasement would be a sign of manic depression – if Isabella were a character in a realistic domestic drama.

Of course she is not. But the fact that she is not should not prevent us from noticing her two most obvious traits of character. First, she is devoid of a sense of humour to an extent that only the most self-important of people can be. Second, the uncertainty lying behind her self-importance is a sign of a fundamental immaturity, an immaturity which accounts for those rapid changes of mood that occur both in her interview with Lucio here and in her two encounters with Angelo at II, ii and II, iv. In the first, she switches over from the excessive self-mistrust of 'Alas! what poor ability's in me . . . ?' to the elated self-confidence of 'soon – I'll send him certain word of my success', in a matter of seconds. In the second (at II, ii) the hesitant, withdrawing manner that makes Lucio despair of her ('too cold, too cold') gives way to over-excitement and the sexually provocative entreaties that drive Angelo mad with lust and desire. The same with Claudio. She will bear whips as rubies and throw her life down as if it were a pin. Probably if she were in Claudio's position she would indulge in the same histrionics. But Claudio, who is one of Shakespeare's rather disappointingly average young men, much prefers a quiet life with Juliet to martyrdom at the altar of his sister's purity. He may be wrong, but at least his language is consistent with the facts. Isabella's whips and rubies are not. There is no question of her actually receiving them. But the discrepancy between what she is and what she thinks she is and says she is does not, in the theatre, make us wonder if she is a manic-depressive or schizophrenic or what have you. It makes us laugh. Isabella, with her stampings and ravings and puttings-up with nasty suggestions and insults, is comic. She is not witty or gay or fanciful like Shakespeare's earlier mature heroines. We don't laugh *with* her. We laugh *at* her. In other words, she is a figure of farce.

As a figure of farce she takes her place in a play much more given over to farce than is often supposed. I don't say the play as a whole is a farce. But it is at least as much a farce as a 'dark comedy' or a 'satiric drama' or a 'drama of ideas'. Look at Claudio's sudden changes and inconsistencies, for example. Or Angelo's: in II, ii he quickly shifts from the position of 'Look, what I will not, that I cannot do' to that of 'It is the law, not I, condemn your brother' – which is to say, 'Look, what I cannot, that I will not do.' Nobody indulges in the knockabout humour we get in *A Comedy of Errors* or *The Taming of the Shrew*, because *Measure for Measure* is what I should call a farce of ideas. Ideas, and the failure of human beings to grasp them and apply them logically, are what trips up the characters. Behaviour on the stage moves in the direction of farce when the actions of the characters become more and more automatic and less and less the calculated issue of their conscious desires and motives. I would suggest that this is more pronounced in *Measure for Measure* than in any other play by Shakespeare except *The Comedy of Errors* and (for completely non-farcical reasons that I shall explain later) *The Tempest*.

The reason is simple. All the characters think they are free to do as they think fit and recognise, on the whole, that they must accept the consequences of their actions. They pride themselves on their decisions. But they are not really free and the decisions they make issue from a patently artificial situation which is not, though they might think it is, of their own contrivance. This is because they are all actors in the Duke's plot. The Duke has created a situation in which certain actions are almost bound to occur. It may be, even, that he knows to whom they are going to occur, since Mariana tells the boy at the beginning of IV, i that the friar 'Hath often still'd my brawling discontent'. For a studious, retiring type he seems to have got to know an awful lot about his subordinates in the government of Vienna. The way he tells Isabella about Mariana's position and how he intends to exploit it (III, i) also leads us to suppose he planned things in much greater detail than we had thought in Acts I–II. Why he has done it remains a mystery. For political reasons, 'to enforce and qualify the laws'? He says so. But by the time he has finished Vienna is as bad as it has ever been. The effect of his action on society is virtually negligible. To expose Angelo? But to what purpose? Whatever else he is, Angelo appears to be a useful subordinate, the perfect bureaucrat, the ideal number two. The Duke may be conducting a little socio-psychological experiment to substantiate his theories about government and repressed sexuality. He may want to do Mariana a good turn. None of these is a sufficient reason. We do better to leave it with the Duke's words to Friar Thomas, that he will divulge 'moe reasons for this action' in due course, i.e. never. The important thing is not *why* he does it but *that* he does it. The effect of this on the structure of the play is worth considering.

After he has handed over the reins of government to Angelo in the first scene, the Duke has no positive effect on the first half of the play, and we see him on only two more occasions before III, i – once with Friar Thomas and once with Juliet and the Provost. Neither of these scenes has any direct bearing on the drama of Acts I–III, involving Isabella and Angelo, and Isabella and Claudio. In the first half of *Measure for Measure*, then, the characters rush into the vacuum the Duke's absence has left, and fill it up with something much like the plot he had predicted from them. And so, as a consequence of the discrepancy that manifestly opens up between their sense of the importance of their actions and our knowledge of how those actions were virtually pre-determined, they are made to act farcically. There is a comic violence and extremism in their behaviour at which we laugh.

Then in the second half of the play (III, i–v, i) the Duke has to re-enter the plot and sort out the complications raised by his previous action. This would be all very well if everything had gone according to plan. In fact, though much has gone as he expected it to (the main developments are as he had predicted), little things get in the way, and little things can make big things go completely off course. Take Angelo. He is every bit as stickling, as mean, as devious and as passionate as the Duke expected him to be. Mariana can enter the plot just where he had intended she should. But unfortunately Angelo turns out to be something else as well. He is cynical enough to decide to decapitate Claudio after all. And one little problem begets another. The Duke can get round the Angelo problem by borrowing somebody else's head. But whose? Well, what about Barnardine's. He's been lying about in the straw for long enough without earning his keep; and he doesn't care whether he lives or dies anyway. But he does. At the eleventh hour he decides he won't die today for any man's persuasion. In the end the Duke gets the head he wants (Ragozine's), and he gets his way with the rest of them. But only after his dashings about the streets and prisons of Vienna have rendered him as farcical as the rest of the characters in the play. He begins to look ridiculous. The more he participates in the farce, the more farcical he becomes. Even the solemnities of Act v are not enough to convince us of his seriousness.

Shakespeare's alterations to the source, and especially his development of the characters of Isabella and the Duke, have the effect of converting much of the story into what I call a farce of ideas. We laugh at the characters' inability to make their all too human actions correspond with the ideas – of the rule of law, of Christian mercy, of justice and of the need for self-sacrifice – that are supposed to govern them. We laugh also at the discrepancy between the characters' insistence on their freedom of action, their power of decision, and the Duke's pre-ordination of the way they will actually behave, the roles they will fulfil. However, I said that *Measure for Measure* as a whole was not a farce – only that what happens in it frequently encourages the kind of response that is appropriate to farce. That response alternates with a totally different one – much more serious and solemn. For another way of interpreting the behaviour of characters whose actions are represented as being less and less their own because they are taken more and more out of their own hands, is in allegorical terms. The stiffer the characters become, the more automatic their behaviour, the more we are encouraged to look at them in this way. Their actions fall into a pattern which, as I have said, is almost pre-ordained. They are therefore symptomatic of human behaviour in general, a paradigm of human existence in its relation to the grand moral absolutes of justice and mercy. There is no question of one aspect of the play modifying the other; of the farcical element, for example, being softened and toned down by the allegorical. They co-exist. The allegorical pattern of the whole is made up of alternately farcical and solemn material; just as in *Troilus and Cressida* the heroic scene is composed of idealism and cynicism in about equal proportions.

The primary colours of farce are distributed in such a way as to compose an allegorical outline, and because the Duke thinks he is in command of the whole situation, he has to make separate contributions to each 'side' of the play. This accounts for the inconsequentiality of his two most impressive speeches. The advice he gives to Claudio at the opening of III, i is stoic–pagan in both tone and content:

> Be absolute for death; either death or life
> Shall thereby be the sweeter. Reason thus with life.
> If I do lose thee, I do lose a thing
> That none but fools would keep. A breath thou art,
> Servile to all the skyey influences,
> That dost this habitation, where thou keep'st
> Hourly afflict. Merely, thou art Death's fool;
> For him thou labour'st by thy flight to shun
> And yet run'st toward him still. Thou art not noble;
> For all th' accommodations that thou bear'st
> Are nurs'd by baseness. Thou art by no means valiant;
> For thou dost fear the soft and tender fork
> Of a poor worm. Thy best of rest is sleep,
> And that thou oft provok'st; yet grossly fear'st
> Thy death, which is no more. Thou are not thyself;
> For thou exists on many a thousand grains
> That issue out of dust. Happy thou art not;
> For what thou hast not, still thou striv'st to get,
> And what thou hast, forget'st. Thou art not certain;
> For thy complexion shifts to strange effects,
> After the moon. If thou art rich, thou'rt poor;
> For, like an ass whose back with ingots bows,
> Thou bear'st thy heavy riches but a journey,
> And Death unloads thee. Friend hast thou none;
> For thine own bowels which do call thee sire,
> The mere effusion of thy proper loins,

Do curse the gout, serpigo, and the rheum,
For ending thee no sooner. Thou hast nor youth nor age,
But, as it were, an after-dinner's sleep,
Dreaming on both; . . .

whereas the speech he makes to the audience a short time afterwards, at the end of III, ii, is hieratic–Christian:

He who the sword of heaven will bear
Should be as holy as severe;
Pattern in himself to know,
Grace to stand, and virtue go;
More nor less to others paying
Than by self-offences weighing.
Shame to him whose cruel striking
Kills for faults of his own liking!
Twice treble shame on Angelo,
To weed my vice and let his grow!
O, what may man within him hide,
Though angel on the outward side!
How many likeness, made in crimes,
Making practice on the times,
To draw with idle spiders' strings
Most ponderous and substantial things!

In the first he speaks as a precipitant of farce. Not only that,
of course: the speech makes its contribution to the speculations
on the meaning of life and death that run through the play and
that are taken up by Claudio later in the same scene. But in so
far as it contributes to the plot, it does so in respect of its farcical
aspect, preparing Claudio for his breakdown in front of Isabella.
In the second speech the Duke has become subdued entirely
to the part he has to play in the allegorical scheme. He has
changed over from the interfering friar to the bearer of Heavenly
Grace. We have to change our focus as he changes his role.

In this 'second' play – the allegorically patterned one –
Angelo, Isabella, Claudio and the others become types of unregenerate man. They are redeemed by the Duke and the super-
human powers he embodies as he intervenes, from outside, on
their behalf. There is no sudden change. The characters have
anticipated the Duke's awareness of their need long before. They

have referred over and over again to the power of grace. Escalus said at the very beginning that Angelo was worthy 'to undergo such ample grace and honour' as the Duke was prepared to bestow on him. The Provost hoped that Heaven would give Isabella 'saving graces' in her interview with Angelo. And Isabella herself believed that none of the insignia of power become the great 'with half so good a grace' as mercy does. In a context of religious imagery, which is stronger in *Measure for Measure* than anywhere else in Shakespeare, the theological force of the word stands out from its merely conventional application. And it is true that grace of a kind does operate through the Duke's manipulation of incident, in such a way as to bring all to rights and redeem the characters at the end.

We have moved from the farcical behaviour of the characters to the source of that behaviour in the Duke's plan, and we have worked back from the Duke's plan to look at the behaviour of the characters in the allegorical light it throws on them. But that light is fitful. We must now work the other way round, to correct the allegorical bias by emphasising the comic behaviour of the Duke. How are we to detach this from the role he plays in the allegory? Is it possible to see the allegory as a function of the comedy, rather than, as before, the other way about? I think we can. And I think one of the characters shows us how it is to be done. That character is Lucio. His position in the play is more important than, at first sight, it appears to be.

Lucio is the most obvious of the devices Shakespeare uses to diminish the seriousness with which we 'take' the Duke as an embodiment of Heavenly Grace. He is the principal instrument whereby the Duke is cut down to size, the only person in the play who refuses to accept the Duke at his own valuation. More than this, he describes the Duke's conduct (conduct that everyone else describes in the most elevated terms) in terms that, though unfavourable, correspond with what we actually see going on. For the Duke, playing about with dead men's heads and thrusting Mariana into Angelo's bed are dressed up in language like 'Craft against vice I must apply'. Ragozine's unexpected demise is 'an accident that heaven provides'. Oddest of all, he intends to hide from Isabella the news that Claudio is still alive until the right dramatic moment, so that he can show how clever he has been by bringing all the rabbits out of the hat at the same time. That's not the way he puts it, of course. He says, 'But I will keep her ignorant of her good,/To make her heavenly comforts of despair.' If it were not for Lucio we might just accept this – as a part of our expectations of Jacobean fifth acts. But Lucio won't have it. He thinks the Duke is an 'old fantastical Duke of dark corners' who would have 'dark deeds darkly answered'. His leaving Vienna in the first place (which Lucio half-believes was 'an infinite distance/From his true-meant design') was 'A mad fantastical trick'. On each occasion Lucio sees what the Duke describes to others in terms (of 'heaven' and 'grace') proper to the allegory, as 'tricks', 'fantasies', 'dark deeds' – in terms proper to farce and comic intrigue.

Lucio's behaviour proclaims him a warmer, less pompous and less self-appraising version of what the Duke himself represents. On the surface the two characters could not be less like each other: the one austere, responsible, highly moral; the other loose-living, irresponsible, not giving a fig for morality. But beneath these superficial differences they stand for the same thing, and it may be that Lucio's greater openness and involvement in the passions of others allows him to stand for it more successfully. At II, iv Angelo had asked, 'Might not there be a charity in sin?' In his case there was not. His words were no more than a hypocritical justification for his evil designs on Isabella. But it may be that what is not true of Angelo's designs is true of Lucio's impulses. For, with the exception of the Provost, Lucio is the one truly charitable character in the play. His dirty joking with the gentlemen during his first appearance gives way to genuine and active concern for Claudio when he hears the news of his imprisonment: 'But after all this fooling, I would not have it so.' He is the man who goes to Isabella and gets her to intervene on Claudio's behalf. He is the man who stops her from giving in after the first minor setback. He is the man who participates at the centre of the human muddle – the prison – which the Duke visits from the outside, as a distant counsellor.

That is why the Duke cannot pardon Lucio at the end. Can it sensibly be argued that Lucio deserves pardon less than Angelo, after what Angelo had intended to do and thought he had done with Claudio and Isabella? Surely not. Lucio's sins, distasteful as they appear to be, are venial by comparison. But he represents two things that diminish the Duke's sense of his own importance and *our* trust in the seriousness of his allegorical role. First, he is a scurrilous gutter voice that refuses to accept the Duke at his own valuation. He converts the appearance of high principle into the reality of low trickery, allowing us to see the Duke's actions in a light no one else has the effrontery to shed on them. Secondly, he represents a kind of grace that the Duke cannot aspire to – though aspire is the wrong word, since the movement is down, not up. Almost the first thing Lucio says is that 'Grace is grace, in spite of all controversy' and he tells Isabella that when maidens sue 'Men give like gods;' i.e. they exercise a kind of grace of their own. But, as William Empson has reminded us in a fine poem, these are 'Ambiguous gifts, as what gods give must be'. There is an incarnate grace alive in human friendship and warmth of feeling that exists at the very centre of corruption, a sort of 'charity in sin' of the kind Angelo unwittingly referred to. The Duke cannot approach it. His transcendent grace is seen through, has doubts cast upon it by Lucio in both his comic and allegorical functions. Whichever way we look at the play, the Duke's standing is compromised and undermined. Little wonder he can't extend his forgiveness to such a man. He knows, and exposes, too much:

> *Lucio*: A shy fellow was the Duke; and I believe I know the cause of his withdrawing.
> *Duke*: What, I prithee, might be the cause?
> *Lucio*: No, pardon; 'tis a secret must be lock'd within the teeth and the lips.

A comic mistake, or a Delphic pronouncement? Either way, it leaves us with a fine balance to weigh who is the wise man and who is the fool.

11

The Winter's Tale

There is little in Shakespeare's last plays that we should have been surprised to have found in his first. His comedies begin and end with an eventful sea journey, the one to a seaport, the other to an island in the Mediterranean. In both cases the journey leads to confusion and then to joy – in the restoration of parent to child and in the repeal of a harsh sentence imposed by one of the characters (in authority at the time) on one or more of the others. Aegeon is as amazed at what he finds in Ephesus as Alonso is at what he finds on Prospero's magic island. Both are places of enchantment. Both harbour a pleasant young girl who will marry the threatened father's son. In spite of his comparative lack of interest in romantic love at the beginning of his career, Shakespeare's early plays have a great deal – in respect of plot, the general outlines of character, and some specific scenes – in common with the later ones. Also, the middle comedies make use of almost all the events that occur in *Pericles*, *Cymbeline*, *The Winter's Tale* and *The Tempest*. Situations that threaten dismay and disaster invariably resolve themselves into concord and harmony. Why, then, do we feel that these last plays are different; that although what is done is familiar, the spirit in which it is done is strange?

The most obvious indication of the difference is that none of these last plays is very funny. The bawds and brothel keepers in *Pericles* hardly seem to be trying – in spite of the opportunities Marina presents them with in the bawdy house. Autolycus is pushed into a corner of the last two acts of *The Winter's Tale* and has nothing with which to amuse himself (or us) there but a few indifferent puns and one delightful song. Stephano and Trinculo in *The Tempest* come a poor second to Sir Toby and Sir Andrew in *Twelfth Night*. Their cakes and ale have come out of the sea-water decidedly heavy and flavourless. Prospero spruced up their clothes for them, but he forgot about their

jokes. Wit is at a discount. So is low comedy, or farce. Imagine
what Shakespeare would have done with Marina in Mytiline
even as early as *The Taming of the Shrew*. Think what he *did*
do for a similar situation in *Measure for Measure*. Isabella's aura
of stainless chastity did not preclude her being laughed at, as
well as felt for, in her scenes with Angelo. Marina's very similar
scenes with Boult and Lysimachus hardly rate a smile. And no
wonder. Even the pandars of *Pericles* worry about the sore terms
they stand upon with the gods. Can you imagine Mistress Over-
done ever allowing such a consideration to enter her head?
Surely not. The fact is that in *Measure for Measure* the heroine
is not taken at her own valuation. In *Pericles* she is. The same
tends to be true of all these later plays – up to a point. That
point is reached in *The Tempest*, where Miranda's role contrasts
strongly with those of Marina and Perdita that come before it.
Prospero controls Miranda here in a way no one controls either
of the earlier heroines. When the princess stops being the un-
witting agency of a mysterious but benevolent chance, and becomes instead the perplexed object of a dramatically enacted
design that *looks* like chance (though not of a benevolent variety),
it is time to call a halt. Symbolism gives way to mere behaviour.
But there is still no comedy, no laughter.

These heroines all take themselves utterly seriously. More
than that, Shakespeare takes them seriously as well – so seriously
that he will not allow their seriousness to be compromised by
over-exposure. Therefore he removes them from the centre and
makes them influence the plot more by what they are than by
what they do. The earlier heroines participated at the centre of
the action. They tended to be the most decisive and effective
people in the play. Only Imogen, in *Cymbeline*, is like that here.
More often the heroines are more acted upon than acting. True,
they are strong-willed and able to stand their ground in the face
of abuse and ill-breeding, rather like the Lady in Milton's
Comus. Miranda is a bit on the pallid side, but she does try to
protect Ferdinand from her father's bad temper, and both
Marina with Lysimachus and Perdita with Polixenes take up
a strong defensive position. Indeed defence of the kind they
offer has a sort of active virtue in it, again like the Lady in
Comus. But it does not precipitate action, it completes an action
already under way. That has been set off by the father, not the

daughter. In these final plays the older generation again usurp the centre. The young have a contribution to make, a very important contribution. But the plot is not theirs. The drama neither springs from them nor revolves around them. They have more in common with their tragic than with their comic sisters.

This is true also of the plays they inhabit. Take *The Winter's Tale*. There are several respects in which it is more like one of Shakespeare's tragedies than his earlier comedies. Unavoidably the first three acts cry out for comparison with *Othello*. The same gnawing jealousy on the part of the protagonist, the same steady repudiation by his guiltless wife of the charges he brings against her. Only Iago is missing – he'd already had a rerun as Iachimo in *Cymbeline*. Leontes' self-inflicted anguish and his stunned remorse when he hears of Hermione's death are perfectly consonant with tragic experience as we have known it from *Othello* to *Timon*. The hero's rhetoric expresses a powerful and dynamic movement of the spirit; the rhythms and imagery with which it proceeds are complex and forceful. Leontes' personality is as powerfully present in the language he speaks and the acts he performs as was Shylock's – but in Leontes' case it is more subtly displayed and it does not have to compete with a romantic environment. That has to wait until Act IV, in which he does not appear. When it is prolonged into Act V, in a different place and with different properties, and Leontes walks into it, his previous absence and the way he left the stage at the end of Act III all prepare him for it. But his behaviour in the first half of the play is not romantic at all. Only with hindsight can it be made to anticipate romance. Because it is part of a tragic action, I do not feel called upon to deal with it here.

My business is to look at the shape of the whole play, from back to front. It ends happily. Therefore in the most widely accepted sense of the word it is a comedy. But the end is hardly implicit in the beginning. Leontes' 'Prithee, bring me/To the dead bodies of my queen and son:/One grave shall be for both' (III, ii) almost completes the tragic action. We might expect the stage direction 'Draws his sword and falls upon it' – a fitting conclusion to the play. But no. Instead, Antigonus reappears with the baby Perdita, lays her down on the sea-shore, and is devoured by the intolerable bear. Enter a shepherd. Romance has arrived, albeit in a somewhat grotesque and bloody habit. We are to stay with it for much of the rest of the play. Time steps on-stage (with petty pace, metrically speaking) and tells us to close our eyes, open them again, and pretend we have slept sixteen years. Interesting that we do not dream. We simply wake from one kind of existence, tragic, to another kind, romantic. Both are waking states. The play is devoid of those perplexing half lights and uncertain fancies that some of the earlier plays and, later, *The Tempest*, are full of.

Scene iv is the crucial one in this transitional fourth act. It is bright day. No mystery, no supernatural interference with the landscape and its flower displays. No chance of hoary-headed frosts falling into the fresh lap of the crimson rose in *this* garden. The seasons do not change their wonted liveries, there has not even been any human interference with the growth of the flowers. Cross-grafting is out. It is the first time we have met Florizel, and the adult Perdita. What do they look like? Dresden? No. Better apply that word to the brightly-decorated and hard-edged figures of the lovers in that other pastoral, *As You Like It*. These are too stately, too grand. Also they are too much flesh and blood. I must be careful about this. Rosalind and Celia in the earlier play are infinitely more lively, more sociable and more wittily civilised. They value their personalities more. Perdita and her lover are much less individual, less interesting. But Perdita especially is more physical. To start with she speaks verse, not prose; and verse of a kind that is difficult to describe. If it were set to music it would be played by a wind instrument, and we should hear the breath underneath the notes. No wonder her blood looks out. Her language is full of references to breeding and bastards, impregnated with knowledge of the body, of sexuality, of the physicality of being. All this quite consistent with her undoubted spiritual and technical ignorance. Perdita's conversation with Polixenes is, to coin a phrase, full and frank. After Cleopatra, she is the Shakespearean heroine I can least comfortably imagine being played by a boy – in spite of her youth, and her reputation among the critics.

That is what iv, iv looks like and sounds like. But what does it say? Its second half is given over almost entirely to the plot. Camillo makes Florizel and Perdita aware of their danger and gets them away to Sicilia, whilst Polixenes mutters about the nasty things he'll do to Perdita when he gets hold of her. But the first half is irrelevant to the plot, full of dancing, scattering flowers about and having elegant and somewhat philosophical conversations about 'great creating nature'. It is a great favourite with the critics, and a gift for stage designers and special effects men – so much so that for well-nigh half a century it has been considered rather bad taste to express doubts about the quality of the contribution it makes to the play. G. Wilson Knight calls the argument about grafting 'a microcosm of the whole play'. D. A. Traversi calls it a perfect example of Shakespeare's symbolic technique, the '*carn*-stem' in 'carnation' having 'a clear connection with the flesh', and the 'streak'd gillyvors', 'bastards' between crude nature and the realm of 'grace'. (As the editor of the Arden edition points out, it is unfortunate for Traversi that 'carnation' is a corruption of the English 'coronation', not a derivative of the Latin 'carnalis' = 'fleshly'. So with these appreciations firmly lodged in my mind, it came as a shock to open D. J. Enright's *Shakespeare and the Students* and find him referring to it as a 'sentimentalised seed-merchant's catalogue'. He thinks that, 'With Shakespeare a little pastoral customarily goes a long way,' and Act IV of *The Winter's Tale* is no exception. Is he right? After the vividly presented drama of Leontes' jealous attack on Hermione and its consequences, does it come not merely as a surprise, but as a let-down too, to find ourselves thrust into the middle of a summer garden and a long conversation about whether it's better to cross-breed flowers or allow them to grow naturally.

One thing we can say right away is that whatever else it may be the whole sequence (IV, iv, 70–167) is a set piece on a traditional theme. The rival claims of nature and art had been argued as early as the third and fourth books of Spenser's *Faerie Queene* and were to be argued about as late as Andrew Marvell's 'The Mower against Gardens' (Pope's 'Epistle to Burlington' is an Augustan variation). Shakespeare has already had a crack at it in the Welsh scenes of *Cymbeline*. There is a great deal of irony in the fact that here Perdita's betrothal to Florizel represents in respect of human beings an indisputable flouting of what she has to say about flowers. Gillyvors are pinks or carnations, and as such the result of interbreeding. So Perdita will not put

> The dibble in earth to set one slip of them;
> No more than were I painted I would wish
> This youth should say 'twere well, and only therefore
> Desire to breed by me.

Unfortunately for the logic of her case, however, their paint is her plainness. So far as she knows, her marriage with Florizel will itself produce 'bastard' offspring – in the sense of the word she favours. Conversely, Polixenes contradicts his own beliefs as they apply to human beings and, specifically, as they apply to Perdita and his son in the second half of the scene. Both characters have strong views. Both of them have no idea of how their views should correspond with their behaviour.

What is gained by their confusion? Maybe Polixenes is testing Perdita (though to what end I cannot fathom). Maybe Perdita's nobility is speaking for her, the real king's daughter who loves the king's son, not the Mistress of the Feast who thinks she loves the rustic Dorcas. At all events, both Perdita and Polixenes are speaking against their own best interests, Polixenes deliberately, Perdita in ignorance of the real identity of her lover. The reversal of the point of view seems to me quite arbitrary. I cannot see that anything is gained by Perdita's demonstration that blood will tell, except a blow for aristocratic interbreeding that is irrelevant to the concerns of this play.

If we discount the argument, we are left with the delightful scene of young people healthily ignoring prohibitions that the old try to impose on them. You would never think so, from what some commentators on the play have said, but it is a *summer* scene. Perdita and Florizel may represent the regenerative powers of spring, coming after the winter's tale of which they are the suffering offspring; but they do not do so against the appropriate seasonal backcloth. The 'gilly' in 'gillyvors' is most probably July – a bit late for pinks, but only by a month at the most. Besides, Perdita admits that the flowers she gives Polixenes are flowers 'Of middle summer'. She has no flowers of spring to give Florizel and Mopsa and the other girls at the feast. Surely what has happened is that Shakespeare has availed himself of the opportunity to present a courtly dialogue with an ironic twist to it, without a great deal of concern for its place in the total narrative. There is a sense in which the revolution of the seasons, the passing of time, and the correspondent powers of art and nature are relevant to *The Winter's Tale*, and it is a very important sense. But it has little to do with breeding and interbreeding, or specifically spring following winter.

What it has to do with has been suggested most convincingly by M. M. Mahood in the essay on *The Winter's Tale* in her *Shakespeare's Wordplay*. In the first three acts of the play Leontes has been presented as a man who has wilfully cut himself off from everything that is wholesome, playful, youthful in the life of nature. His bitter comments on Mamillius's playfulness, and his insistence that those comments are appropriate to his mother's behaviour ('thy Mother plays'), force him into a wild belief that he too is playing a part, 'so disgrac'd a part', which he resents and deplores. The two meanings of 'play', playing games and playing a part in a play, combine to increase Leontes' rancour and intensify his jealousy: 'Unable to play in the sense of refreshing himself from the non-moral and instinctive life of childhood, Leontes begins to play in the sense of constructing an intensely moral drama in which he acts the role of the deceived husband.' In the sheep-shearing scene we are returned to the 'non-moral and instinctive life of childhood'. Perdita's role in it is to represent just such as cross-grafting (in her case of gentle birth and country upbringing) as she is deploring in her conversation with Polixenes. Restored to her father, she brings with her the innocent playfulness Leontes enjoyed in his childhood games with Polixenes ('twinn'd lambs that did frisk i' th' sun'), but which he lost somewhere during the first hundred lines of the second scene of the play.

I should be as happy with this interpretation of Perdita's role if the cross-grafting speeches didn't exist. Neither the ironies nor the solemnities of her little scene with Polixenes seem to me to be at all appropriate to the position she occupies in the symbolic scheme of the play which Professor Mahood so accurately describes. As I shall explain below, I think that further complications are produced by the fact that in this long pastoral scene as a whole, terms of art and nature are used which are used again in the statue scene in Act v. But the functions of the terms appear to have little to do with one another. The nature that attends on Perdita's behaviour among the shepherds has little in common with the nature that breathes through the statue Hermione has become at Leontes' court. And Perdita's disguise as the princess of the feast has as little in common with Hermione's as a statue: the ironic appropriateness of the one has no correspondence with the more symbolically and hieratically effective presence of the other. Leaving aside Professor Mahood's acceptable demonstration of connections which *do* exist, too much of the pastoral scene appears to be establishing connections with the rest of the play without actually doing so. But more of this below.

Roughly speaking there are two kinds of approaches you are likely to encounter in reading about *The Winter's Tale*. The first is represented at its best by Northrop Frye in his Bampton Lectures on the comedies, collected under the title *A Natural Perspective*. He likes to pass beyond the detail of what is actually happening in the plays – the characters' behaviour, the immediate sense of what they say and do – to the generic pattern that lies behind it. As a result, character is often reduced to a role and the movement of the play is conceived as the working-out of a design inherent in the genre to which it belongs. Sometimes it seems that Shakespeare's handling of the basic story – the additions he makes to it and the detail he applies to it – is good only in so far as it allows somebody like Northrop Frye to come along and strip it down to its bare essentials again.

I am being unfair. But the exaggeration brings out the dangers inherent in such a procedure. For Professor Frye *The Winter's Tale* is a play that symbolises the way the reviving force of nature irresistibly pushes life forward and transforms the sterile past into a fruitful present. In T. S. Eliot's words from 'The Dry Salvages', 'Time the destroyer is time the preserver.' Everything in the play has to be made to fall into this pattern since the movement must be displayed at every stage in its development. Antigonus's exit pursued by a bear can't have been put in just because the Globe managed to get the loan of a bear from the bear-garden across the way. There is no question of the bear being one of the 'old gags' Louis MacNeice enumerated in 'Autolycus', his witty poem about this play. ('Its mainsprings were old gags – babies exposed,/Identities confused' etc.) No. It all has to fit: 'part one ends with a clown hearing the cries of Antigonus as the bear tears out his shoulder bone; part two begins with the same clown hearing the cries of Autolycus pretending that his shoulder blade is out.' There is just one little local difficulty for those of us who attend to the details. Part two doesn't *begin* with the same clown hearing the cries of Autolycus. As well as the shepherd and the clown ending part one, and Time bridging the gap with his feeble couplets, there is a little scene between Polixenes and Camillo, and Autolycus's song about the daffodils. This, incidentally, turns out to be the lyric balance in the second half of the play to Mamillius's story about the man who dwelt by a churchyard in the first. Unfortunately we are not in a position to verify this puzzling supposition because Mamillius never told his story. When critics come to their conclusions about a play's meaning by advancing information as to what is *not* in it I think we can safely say that their case is not proven.

The Winter's Tale is particularly vulnerable to this sort of symbolic interpretation, and the danger now is that people will bend over backwards to prove that it isn't symbolic at all; or where it is, it is bad. This usually means that Acts I–III are splendid (which they are) but that the pastoral scenes in Act IV and the statue scene in Act V are poor stuff. Victorian and Edwardian readers usually thought along these lines, though they had a soft spot for Perdita's nosegay. Some recent commentators have been disposed to agree with them. D. J. Enright has put their case most vigorously. He admires the first three acts, deplores the fourth, and finds the fifth unaccountably impressive. 'That the "happy ending" of *The Winter's Tale* is right is the result of other parts of the play being what, in conjunction, they are. The artistic logic which brings us lawfully to this ending is too delicate, too complex, for analysis.' i.e. he doesn't know how it happens. But surely if three acts are good, and a fifth one is also good, though in a different way, might it not be sensible to suppose that the fifth is as good as it is because the fourth has prepared for it to be so? Enright doesn't want to admit that, because it goes against the grain of his common-sensical attitude towards people's behaviour in the play. What's good enough for Leontes and Hermione ought to be good enough for Florizel and Perdita. Since it is obviously not, and they insist on speaking a romantic verse that is quite alien to the mood of the play before their arrival in it, Shakespeare's reliance on them must have been mistaken. They can't possibly be capable of bridging the gap between tragedy and an autumnal romance.

I am afraid my own view on the unity of *The Winter's Tale* is heretical. Frye and Enright, differently as they approach the play, have in common a conviction of its completeness, its homogeneity, its overall artistic logic. However mysteriously, everything hangs together. I don't think it does. It seems to me that *The Winter's Tale* is, in everything but its plotting, three separate works of art. The first part of it is obviously of a piece in every respect – an almost complete tragic action in three acts. The fourth act is almost completely divorced from everything around it. Even Polixenes with his sadistic and Machiavellian intrigue, is a different man from the one he was earlier. Polixenes' reflections on nature and art have encouraged critics to suppose that there is some connection between what he says here and what Paulina and Leontes say about what appears to be the same subject in Act v. But there isn't any connection. Polixenes' speech is part of a debate on art and nature which, with the exception noted above, is restricted to this scene. It is so densely packed that we have to read it several times before we can construe its meaning, and when we have so done so it tells us nothing that is germane to Hermione's performance as a statue. This is an effective device to slow down Leontes' recognition of his good fortune and to save Hermione the trouble of responding. What would she say? Shakespeare had had the same trouble with Thaisa in *Pericles*, and she was allowed first to swoon, then to explain what had happened to her (how she became a priestess of Diana). Now the last thing we saw Hermione do before she returned in Act v was, precisely, to swoon. That was understandable – but she mustn't be allowed to do it again. She is not fundamentally the swooning type. The alternative is to tell Leontes what she has been doing for the past sixteen years, and once that is out of the bag – knitting with Paulina? – the whole solemn, almost mystical atmosphere of the act is lost. The last thing we want to think about is what she could possibly have been *doing*.

The story of *The Winter's Tale*, as Shakespeare received it from Robert Greene's *Pandosto: The Triumph of Time*, demanded that sixteen years elapse between Hermione's 'death' and the restoration of Perdita and Hermione to Leontes. A writer for the stage could avoid having Leontes (Pandosto) kill himself and Hermione (Fawnia) really die, but there was no way of getting round the passage of those sixteen years. The problem was a theatrical one. There is no question of an obstacle being placed in the way of Shakespeare's intention to deal with matters that interested him: in all the late plays he was evidently preoccupied with the way time restores as well as destroys. The difficulty lay in the fact that time is the dramatist's friend in small quantities but his enemy in large ones. Shakespeare was not writing a novel. Therefore he could not show the events of those sixteen years occurring step by step or with long recapitulatory passages of narrative. They had to be shown in a series of dramatic exchanges and romantic revelations. But these must not be too sudden, especially if a large gap of time is supposed to intervene. Surely the pastoral scene is so long because Shakespeare wants to get us used to a different way of approaching human behaviour from the tragic one he had favoured in the first three acts. The sombre dignity of Leontes' behaviour in Act v, and Hermione's pose as a statue, have something in common with both the passionate individuation of Acts i-iii and the abstracted calm of Act iv. By making what he does make of Act iv, Shakespeare must have hoped to establish the appropriate mood for the scene of reconciliation that was to follow. He succeeded. But in the process he did two confusing things. He introduced the red herring of the art/nature debate in scene iv, making it seem all the more important by signalling its ironic application, in the restricted sense, to Florizel and Perdita themselves. Then, in Act v, he presented another picture of art and nature cooperating in a tableau of enormous dramatic power. However, Paulina's magic (which is 'an art/Lawful as eating') is a concern of the last act alone. Though art completes nature, and releases it from a restraint that the passage of time renders no longer necessary, it does so rather surprisingly and with little but a theatrical justification. In his next play, by telescoping rather than expanding time, Shakespeare found a way out of the difficulty and invented an action in which the coincidence of art and nature was insisted upon throughout.

12

The Tempest

The Tempest was Shakespeare's last comedy and almost certainly the last play he wrote without the collaboration of others. It is one of those works of art that suffer from the familiarity we feel with them. We read it as schoolchildren; we have probably seen several productions of it; its sea-changes and brave new worlds and our being such stuff as dreams are made of have entered into common usage. We are probably not aware of how strange it is. The only other play in which supernatural beings take major parts, *A Midsummer Night's Dream*, impresses by cleverness as much as by enchantment. *The Tempest* is not an obviously clever play. It is haunting – full of strange echoes half heard and less than half remembered. Works of art of this kind are very difficult to talk about. They encourage either a vaguely 'poetic' response, or explanations that shift very rapidly and often imperceptibly into creative perversions of whatever meaning the work in question actually possesses. The title recalls, quite circumstantially, Giorgione's 'Tempesta', another of these mysterious creations that cry out to the onlooker to complete them by providing an explanation of their strangeness. And like Giorgione's painting, Shakespeare's play resists explanation. The column and the stream of the picture, the melodies and visions of the play, are the more powerfully alive to the imagination for being parts of a whole that is whole by virtue of nothing we can finally explain. We can plot their iconography and track down their sources, we can sound what stops we please; but we cannot pluck out the heart of their mystery.

All the same, many have tried to get at the heart of *The Tempest*. Where they have been unable to discover its secrets in the play Shakespeare wrote, they have gone behind the play to compose parallel actions, sequels, explanatory variations on the theme and its subjects. W. H. Auden wrote a medley of verse and prose called *The Sea and The Mirror* in which each of the principal

characters of *The Tempest* tries to explain himself in cryptic
soliloquy. T. S. Eliot allowed echoes of the play to wind their way
through his most puzzling poem, *The Waste Land.* Humbler
critics have discovered allegorical patterns of various kinds just
beneath the surface of the drama. But it is no use. The secret of
The Tempest refuses to disclose itself. I shall not try to disclose it.
Instead I shall try to show how the explanations we are
encouraged to provide fall apart as they brush up against the
props and the poetry of the play world we have entered.

Let us enter the play at its ending, or almost at its ending.
Prospero is speaking to Ariel after Caliban, Trinculo and
Stephano have been driven out by the spirit hunters. All his
enemies lie at his mercy (v, i).

Prospero: Now does my project gather to a head.
My charms crack not, my spirits obey; and time
Goes upright with his carriage. How's the day?
Ariel: On the sixth hour; at which time, my lord,
You said our work should cease.
Prospero: I did say so,
When first I rais'd the tempest. Say, my spirit,
How fares the King and's followers?
Ariel: Confin'd together
In the same fashion as you gave in charge,
Just as you left them; all prisoners, sir,
In the line-grove which weather-fends your cell.
They cannot budge till your release. The King,
His brother, and yours, abide all three distracted,
And the remainder mourning over them,
Brimful of sorrow and dismay; but chiefly,
Him you term'd, sir, 'the good old lord Gonzalo';
His tears run down his beard, like winter's drops
From eaves of reeds. Your charm so strongly works 'em
That if you now beheld them your affections
Would become tender.
Prospero: Dost thou think so, spirit?
Ariel: Mine would, sir, were I human. ✓
Prospero: And mine shall.
Hast thou, which are but air, a touch, a feeling
Of their afflictions, and shall not myself,

One of their kind, that relish all as sharply,
Passion as they, be kindlier moved than thou art?
Though with their high wrongs I am struck to th' quick,
Yet with my nobler reason 'gainst my fury
Do I take part; the rarer action is
In virtue than in vengeance; they being penitent,
The sole drift of my purpose doth extend
Not a frown further. Go release them, Ariel;
My charms I'll break, their senses I'll restore,
And they shall be themselves.
Ariel: I'll fetch them, sir.

Having made his decision Prospero abjures his magic, breaks his staff, and becomes a man as other men. It is a scene we have grown used to in the late plays, and magic frequently accompanies it.

The final plays usually end on a note of reconciliation and restitution. In *Pericles*, Marina and Thaisa are restored to the Prince; in *Cymbeline*. Posthumus is restored to Imogen and the King to his counsellor and two sons; and in *The Winter's Tale*, wife, daughter and friend are all restored to Leontes. These events repeat in greater detail and on a wider canvas, the events with which middle comedies like *Much Ado about Nothing*, *As You Like It*, even *All's Well that Ends Well*, concluded. They hark back to the very beginning of Shakespeare's career – to *The Comedy of Errors* and the coming together at the end of that play of Aegeon, his wife and two sons after many years' separation. There, the framework of romance consorted uneasily with the farcical picture it enclosed; and the middle comedies seldom evinced much interest in the reconciliation process, choosing to make use of it as the occasion for festive celebration and display. But in *Pericles* and *The Winter's Tale* the stages by which what has been lost is found are lovingly dwelt upon. The act of reconcilement is – in both word and gesture – ceremonial. Prospero's decision here at the opening of the last act of *The Tempest* augurs the same for what is to come. The rest of the act, however, defies augury. What takes place is not so much a scene of reconciliation as a grudging parley, a sort of pragmatic compromise. Prospero is no Hermione. Twelve years meditating revenge have left their mark. It is important that we were never told what Hermione was meditating in the sixteen years that elapsed between the two halves of *The Winter's Tale*. Prospero belongs to a different area of the folk imagination from Hermione. It is a less fanciful place, more realistic and leaving more reminders of what came before and is to come after.

The ceremonial nature of the last scenes of the later comedies before *The Tempest* can be made to emphasise the artificiality and unlikeliness of what happens in them. Dr Johnson thought that they should convince any audience of the 'unresisting imbecility' of these plays, and Lytton Strachey took them as evidence of Shakespeare's 'dotage' after the period of the great tragedies had run its course. In fact Shakespeare is well aware of the impression he is making. On at least three separate occasions in the last act of *The Winter's Tale* he draws attention to the artificiality of what is going on in words like the second gentleman's on the finding of Perdita: 'This news' he says, 'which is called true, is so like an old tale that the verity of it is in strong suspicion.' We have seen how like an old tale the action of the whole play is, and we have the title to remind us of it. Shakespeare is emphasising the way the reconciliation has to be fabricated; and then proceeding to justify it, to prove it true, by the way he organises the statue scene. The reality of the perfect ending is supposed to triumph over the charges of make-believe and wishful thinking that Shakespeare himself has made. It is also supposed to triumph over the very powerful scepticism that has entered into our thinking about these things as a consequence of our knowledge of Hermione's wasted years and Mamillius's death – of which we are forcibly reminded throughout. The result is an overlaying of plot on pattern. A sense of loss is allowed to persist as a faint shadow that sets off the pattern of reconciliation with which the play closes. A thin band of darkness frames the picture we see, of radiant joy that spreads from the centre almost to the very edges of the frame. It is a testament to the vague unease that will not be altogether tidied away, the ghost of loss that hovers on the fringes of a perfected joy.

In *The Tempest* this shadow flickers across the picture of Prospero's meeting with his brother and his former courtiers, producing as much dark as light. In the passage I have quoted there are two peculiarities about Ariel's message to Prospero and Prospero's reply to it. Ariel says that Alonso, Antonio and Sebastion are 'distracted' – 'all three distracted' are his words. He clearly means that they are as 'Brimful of sorrow and dismay' as the others who mourn them, for it is on the basis of this information that he tells Prospero that in his position he would have pity on them. But if we cast our minds back to the scene (III, iii) in which Ariel saw them last, we shall find that their behaviour doesn't justify his saying what he has said. Gonzalo's word for them is 'desperate'. He means that all of them are responding to the awakening of a sense of guilt for their past crimes, and I think this is true. But they respond differently. Alonso sees the connection between the loss of his son Ferdinand now and his treatment of his brother Prospero twelve years ago, and he is filled with remorse. Antonio and Sebastian do not and are not. They go off together in an aggressive mood, expecting to fight back at the fiends that plague them, by taking them on one at a time. That is a very different kind of desperation to the one Gonzalo meant.

Prospero takes Ariel at his word and assumes, like Gonzalo, that they are all 'penitent'. Ariel has given him no proper grounds for supposing that they are so. By using one word – 'distracted' – to describe the different reactions they made to what happened to them on the island, he has given a grossly misleading impression of the true state of affairs. Alonso is the only one who is distracted into remorse. The other two are as evil and as dangerous as they ever were. A real situation, in which all three of them are 'distracted' and 'desperate', and only one of them is 'penitent', has been transformed by Prospero, with the sympathetic connivance of Ariel, into an imaginary situation in which all are penitent and therefore satisfactorily playing the parts he has allotted to them in his plot. No wonder the whole drift of his purpose extends not a frown further. But in restoring their senses and bringing them to themselves he is not going to perpetuate a miraculous condition of brotherly love and handshakes all round. There never was such a condition, inside or outside the magic circle he has drawn. As he knows well enough himself, he has no power to change the hearts of men. His supposition that in this case he has done so, even if indirectly, is mere wishful thinking.

Prospero's conduct is out of line with what has really happened before the opening of the fifth act. It is also out of line with what he himself is to do after it. In *Cymbeline* and *The Winter's Tale* the subsidiary characters were allowed to participate in the restoration of concord at the close. The villain, Iachimo, was forgiven by Posthumus; and Paulina shook off the restraint of the dead Antigonus and was betrothed to Camillo. Nothing of the sort happens at the end of *The Tempest*. True, Prospero does forgive Antonio and Sebastian as well as Alonso, but in what a grudging spirit: 'I do forgive thee,/Unnatural though thou art.' I have to do it to provide the kind of ending all these good people expect, but don't suppose I enjoy it – is the sort of thing he is saying. 'At this time I will tell no tales.' But what I do at another time is my own business. The manner of his forgiving spoils its matter. So does the villains' acceptance of it. No profuse words of gratitude, as there were with Iachimo. Instead, a spiteful silence in reply to Prospero, and three or four speeches aside or to each other which are predictably churlish, sarcastic, completely unregenerate. What we are given in *The Tempest* is up to a point what we got in *The Winter's Tale*: a 'formal' ending in which that pattern is blurred and made to seem uncertain. But the main difference lies in the dramatically *present*, 'on-stage', recalcitrance of at least two of the characters concerned, and the half-heartedness of the protagonist in the face of such recalcitrance. We are not left merely to speculate on what remains irredeemably 'wrong' *in the past*.

There is another peculiarity about the reconciliation scene. Prospero says he will take the part of his nobler reason against his fury and behave in a spirit of virtue rather than of anger. He will go no further with his purpose. But what was his purpose? Prospero seems to contradict himself. In Act I he tells Miranda that he has done nothing but in care of her. On the other hand in Act IV he congratulates himself on having all his enemies at his mercy. Are we to assume that he is inclined to be merciful and has engineered the shipwreck to produce a situation in which the reconciliations of the last act will be able to take place? That would tally with what he says in Act I. He is obviously very fond of Miranda, and we might suppose that one of the greatest advantages of getting the party from Milan on to his island would be to provide a well-born, well-mannered and attractive young fellow like Ferdinand for her to marry. Or are we to assume that Prospero is bent on revenge? His irascibility and rough behaviour proclaim him to be a very different man from the studious humanist who was thrown out of his library by Antonio and Alonso many years ago. He is obviously smarting under a sense of injured merit and usurped degree quite sufficient to explain his outbursts of rage and threats of dire punishment. Prospero's motives remain obscure. On the whole, though, before these words to Ariel at v, i, I believe we have been inclined to think he will let off his brother, at any rate, with a caution. The way he goes back on what now appears to have been a serious intention, comes as something of a surprise. I cannot think he is indulging in a pretence to test Ariel – the only possible explanation that is consistent with the way he has behaved up to this point.

His behaviour, along with his lack of motive for it and his changes of mood and attitude, remind me of no one so much as the Duke in *Measure for Measure*. In both cases we are watching a man who possesses powers of life and death over the other characters, and who more or less plots the course of their behaviour. Prospero seems to be a development of this character, and his double motive, or lack of motive, can be explained in much the same way. There is one difference. In my chapter on *Measure for Measure*, I traced the way in which our attitude to the Duke keeps changing from one that is appropriate to his role as the allegorical representation of the power of grace to another that is appropriate to his quite different role as a somewhat absurd figure of farce. Prospero also plays two roles, but his performance in one of them receives very much greater emphasis than his performance in the other. His 'stage manager' powers are altogether more highly developed than the Duke's. He is much more in control of the situation. Prospero's white magic and his command over Ariel prevent him from descending to the depths the Duke reached in Act IV of *Measure for Measure*. On the other hand, the time limit set for Ariel's release makes it necessary, or at least expedient, for him to act quickly, and this provides him with plenty of opportunity to display, along with his undoubted dignity, an innate pomposity and a choleric temperament.

His more human side, the disappointed old man hidden inside the demiurge, comes out most strongly in his behaviour towards Ariel. We had a hint of it in his talk to Miranda in I, ii, though I believe we make too much of it there because we want to absolve our author from the charge of tediousness: actually

Shakespeare, as well as Prospero, is a little tedious in this long and not very inspired piece of exposition. But when Prospero has done with it and Ariel comes along to remind him of his promise, the dialogue picks up. It is obviously absurd to call Ariel a 'malignant thing', and equally absurd to have created a situation in which this sort of insult is rendered necessary. Caliban is the real malignant thing, and it is about Caliban that they go on to talk – an obvious example of the time factor getting on Prospero's nerves and obscuring his better judgement. It is the same in IV, i, after the masque. Prospero has forgotten all about Caliban's plot to bash his head in with a log. His sudden remembrance of it throws him into a fit of bad temper – 'Never till this day/Saw I him touched with anger so distempered', says Miranda – but he is no sooner inflamed than he is calmed again. Immediately afterwards he confers with Ferdinand on the insubstantial pageant of life, apologising for his vexation and weakness in a manner uncharacteristic both in its courteousness and its humility.

Our glance at the passage from v, i, together with the complications that arise when we try to 'place' it within the plot of the play, goes to show one thing. No sooner does a pattern seem to be emerging from the obscurity than something comes along to shake it up, to make it incomplete and uncompleteable. As in all the late comedies the movement of the drama, in broad outline, is from loss and destruction to reconciliation, healing, harmony. How and why this movement happens is in the last analysis inexplicable. There are explanations, but they are incomplete. Ferdinand is utterly bemused by his strange mixture of good and ill fortune, a father lost and a bride discovered. As he carries his log on to the stage at III, i he enunciates the theme of the play with his remark that 'most poor matters/Point to rich ends.' They do indeed. But we know, as he does not, that this has not befallen by chance. Prospero determined which the poor matters should be, and predicated the rich ends that they should point to. He could do this, however, only when the fates allowed. The arrival of Alonso and his company in his territorial waters was an 'accident most strange'. 'I find', he says in I, ii, 'my zenith doth depend upon/A most auspicious star', and goes on to emulate Brutus on the tide in the affairs of men which taken at the flood leads on to fortune. In his case it is literally a tide. He can have others take it at the flood, but he cannot, even with his magic

powers, create it. That is the business of the auspicious star, and
he has no control over the heavenly bodies – only the tiny area of
his enchanted island.

Whatever issues are resolved are resolved by a combination of
chance and design. Accidental good fortune bears down upon the
protagonist from outside and he cooperates with it to bring about
a condition of peace and concord which affects every character
in the play. This happens in every one of the late comedies, but
the one that exerts itself most to make the pattern clear is *Cymbeline*. It is studded with little gnomic utterances that sum up the
matter of all these plays. 'Some falls are means the happier to
arise'; 'Fortune brings in some boats that are not steered';
'Many dream not to find, neither deserve,/And yet are steep'd in
favours.' The lines are spoken by Lucius, Pisanio, and Posthumus. They could apply to several characters and events in *The
Tempest*. The difference makes itself felt not in the pattern which
these aphorisms describe, but in the material the pattern is woven
out of. Rich ends remain rich, but the poverty out of which they
have emerged makes itself felt more and more pressingly. In
Pericles and *Cymbeline* things turn out almost entirely for the
best, and there is no suggestion of incompleteness or fragility
about the harmony that has been achieved. But in *The Winter's
Tale* we feel more strongly the sense of wasted years, and the
wistful half-identification of Florizel and Mamillius is a reminder
of what has been sacrificed to the restoration of concord. Then in
The Tempest, there is a persistent, chastening sense of uncertainty. We are aware that, though precarious, this is the most
satisfactory conclusion that can be expected.

This is because many of the details of the plot work against its
overall direction. They insist on petty selfishness, obstinacy, recalcitrance, and the temporary nature of the equilibrium that has
been or is to be established. Take the old lord Gonzalo, for
instance. He is on the whole an admirable man – inclined to take
himself and his ideas over-seriously, but that is a small fault when
set beside his loyalty and strong sense of duty to Prospero. During
the shipwreck in the first scene his reaction to the danger is to
express deep piety tinged with an irrepressible instinct for self-
preservation. 'The wills above be done', he says, 'but I would
fain die a dry death.' A solemn subjunctive trust in the gods and
a selfish hope that he will be spared all the same. Later, when he

is out of danger and able to weigh up the situation in a spirit of detachment, he rejoices 'Beyond a common joy' because all the King's party, himself included, found themselves 'When no man was his own'. This is more a pious hope than a statement of fact. Alonso is the only person to undergo a radical and altogether desirable change of character. Otherwise everybody has been very much his own, and as often as not unpleasantly so. These little traps and pitfalls litter *The Tempest*. Miranda's apostrophe to the brave new world didn't require Aldous Huxley to show how out of touch it was with reality. Prospero replies with a tolerant shrug of the shoulders, ' 'Tis new to thee'. Although the revelation of Ferdinand and Miranda playing chess makes a pretty picture, the 'wrangling' and 'playing false' that go on in it provide a salutary foretaste of life outside the frame.

The detail takes the form of quibble after quibble, fatal little Cleopatras that make the play stumble, not glide, into a harmony that scarcely justifies the effort. Let us turn now to the larger outline, the pattern itself. We shall find it has a strangeness of its own that marks it off from any other of Shakespeare's plays and emphasises the oddness of the detail out of which it is made.

The first thing that strikes us is surely its peculiar alternation of movement and stillness. I suppose it is to be expected that in a play with a plot like this one, Prospero must appear as the still centre of a turning world. He calmly instructs; and Ariel, Caliban and later Ferdinand *do* things. Ariel's restless movements especially contrast with Prospero's composure. He is forever flaming amazement and dancing about his inactive master. But outside of Prospero the characters are often struck rigid into symbolic postures. They are halted and emblematised within his magic circles. Ferdinand in movement composes a picture for Miranda to see when she advances the 'fringed curtain' of her eye. It is as if the eye opens on a scene specially composed for it and wakened into life by Prospero's hieratic injunction. Later Ferdinand and Miranda are discovered playing chess in an equally formal and theatrical composition. It is like the projection of a film that stops at the most significant moments to let the eye take in everything of importance before it is set in motion again and the story is allowed to continue. The slow motion of the last act of *The Winter's Tale* had been entirely frozen – over a shorter period, but on more occasions. This was in keeping with the more diffusely, and therefore less impressively, climactic design of that play.

Then there is the play's compartmentalised structure. I borrow a phrase from Anne Righter's interesting introduction to the Penguin edition of *The Tempest*. She notices the impression of self-containment the scenes produce, and their lack of developing sequence. 'Actions' seem to come to nothing, in the short term at any rate. She proceeds with her argument by recourse to a painterly comparison – a habit I have noticed the play encourages:

> As in the paintings of Piero della Francesca, the eyes even of people confronting each other directly in conversation do not seem to meet. Instead, the lines of sight stray off at angles. There is a puzzling obliquity of vision. The coming together of all the characters at the end, a meeting so long expected, only serves to stress the essential lack of relationship in ways that have an overtone of tragedy.

She must be referring to the Urbino 'Flagellation', and it is true that this does give an accurate impression of one aspect of the play. Vision is peculiarly relative. The separate groups go off in separate directions. But not only that. Within the single group the characters seem to be so cut off from one another that they experience quite different things, or they experience the same things in different ways. They even perceive things differently. In II, i Gonzalo finds that the garments of the ship-wrecked courtiers are not stained with salt water but are 'new dyed' (as Ariel had made them). Nobody else seems to think so. Antonio and Sebastian are distinctly unimpressed. In the same scene Antonio and Sebastian hear bulls and lions bellowing and roaring, but Alonso hears nothing. This is a comic version since Antonio and Sebastian are merely covering up their murderous intent, caught as they are with daggers drawn and 'ghastly looking'. All the same, it points in the same direction.

Like the people in them, the plots don't interact. They run on almost parallel lines, glancing off one another from time to time when they get too close, rather than intersecting with and affecting one another. The two main plots that are allowed to run their course within Prospero's own are almost identical, mirroring each other rather than providing opportunities for contrast and comparison. Antonio and Sebastian want to kill Alonso. Caliban, Trinculo and Stephano want to kill Prospero. But the reflection doesn't end here. The mirror faces back in time as well as across in space. Twelve years ago several of these characters played out the same story, though they took up different roles. Antonio and Alonso had plotted to kill Prospero: Prospero spends much of Act I telling us about this in some detail. So, the plot of *The Tempest* takes the form of three variations on a single action, an action which is, incidentally, the most widely distributed in the whole of Shakespearean drama – namely the plot to kill the king. It is the principal action in *Julius Caesar, Hamlet* and *Macbeth*. And it is rampant throughout the history plays. Furthermore, we follow the progress of this triple plot at the same time as we are made aware of another proto-typical Shakespearean situation – that of young lovers obstructed by the unreasoning prejudice of a possessive parent: *Two Gentlemen of Verona, Romeo and Juliet, The Merchant of Venice, Othello, The Winter's Tale*, and so on. All Shakespearean life is here.

In *The Tempest*, however, none of these things need be taken seriously. Prospero was saved from the fate intended for him, and he came safely to the island with Miranda. As for the present plots, we know Prospero is in control of the situation and does not intend that he, or any other innocent person, shall come to harm. The king who knows the plot (indeed in a sense he can be said to have created it) will not be killed. Ariel is there to see to it that what is intended as evil bears good fruit: Alonso cannot be made to repent, but he can be manoeuvred into a position where he can choose to do so – at the same time as the plot he created twelve years ago is reconstructed and applied against himself. Prospero also controls Ferdinand and Miranda, but his obstruction of their betrothal turns out to be no less benevolent than that of Portia's dead father was in *The Merchant of Venice*. He is determined only that they shall abide the time, when the prize will be no longer light (I, ii) and when Ferdinand's rediscovery of his father will provide the occasion for a reconciliation of the parents. The endemically or potentially tragic situations of the earlier plays are reduced to manageable proportions. Prospero's benevolent purpose extends to them all, and is seen to do so by the audience from the start. There is no suspense as to what the outcome will be, only as to how and when it will be achieved.

'When' is most important. There is no reason, as far as I can see, why it should be; but Prospero thinks it is, and so it is. He never tires of pointing out to Miranda and Ariel how little time he has to exercise his power over the shipwrecked lords. The arrival of his brother and the rest of the Neapolitan court in the vicinity of the island is a stroke of luck he must not fail to make good use of, and quickly. He is always asking the time of day, how much has been done, how much there is to do. Both Ariel and himself must spend 'the time twixt six and now... most preciously' (I, ii); 'ere suppertime [he] must perform/Much business; and from IV, i onwards he allows himself to become more and more aware of the time when his labours will end, now his project has gathered to a head. With *The Comedy of Errors*, *The Tempest* is the only one of Shakespeare's plays which comes anywhere near observing the so-called classical unity of time. Everything happens in the space of less than twenty-four hours. But, as usual, there is a difference. In *The Comedy of Errors* the rapidity with which one action followed another made us hold our breath. We were seldom reminded of the greater time span into which the lesser one fitted, and so both the playwright and ourselves had to make the most of the time, the only time, we had – as usual with farce. Quite the reverse with *The Tempest*. In spite of its narrow time span and its brevity, the play never seems breathless. There are two 'planes' of time set against each other in it. The impression we get is of a vast span of time narrowing into the space of a few hours, of the 'dark backward and abysm of time' reflected as on a clock's face as the minute hand moves rapidly over its surface.

What happens in *The Tempest* impresses us as being only a small part of a much larger action extending far into space and time, to Claribel in Tunis and to the usurpation of Prospero's dukedom twelve years ago that is repeated now in the two plots, against Alonso and himself. At this moment and only at this moment, all these events are capable of entering into harmony – and so Shakespeare seizes on such a moment to make his play, and Prospero seizes on it to restore himself to his country, reconcile himself with his brother, and marry his daughter to a most suitable young man. These moments come rarely, and when they come they come through a grace that has nothing to do with the character's own initiative or deserving, and for a very short time. That must be why Prospero, in spite of his magic powers, and in spite of his stillness and (interrupted) composure, is in a hurry. In that short time things assume their 'ideal' proportions and relations to one another. Processes of time, mediated by a human agency such as Prospero is represented as being, fall magically into a kind of order – compromised by human error and ingratitude, but for the moment almost perfect, as near perfect as can be hoped for, and with hopeful issue.

The reality of the state of grace is doubtful, a temporary and aesthetic illusion: like a play (*The Tempest*) or like a masque (Iris, Ceres and Juno), it is 'baseless' and 'insubstantial', existing only on an enchanted island for a moment of time. Nevertheless, like the experience in the wood outside Athens of *A Midsummer Night's Dream*, it can have a permanent effect on those it has touched. Within a short time Ferdinand has proved himself 'patient' in his love for Miranda. The lovers' experience of each other on the island promises to 'grow to something of great constancy' in the brave new world beyond.

This has remained one of the final, mysterious paradoxes of Shakespeare's art. Every precipitant of tragic action has its comic and healing complement. A handkerchief, dropped at a careless moment, can provoke a bloodbath. But a fairy quarrel can lead to a wedding; and a few hours on a magic island can lead to another wedding. Shakespeare shows how it is possible 'To draw with idle spider's strings/Most ponderous and substantial things'. Neither of these comic events is explicable to common sense. Both of them are fantastic, unjustifiable in terms other than those of art. But dramatically, as metaphors of experience, they are true, they make sense. As usual, *Cymbeline* has the pithiest way of saying it and, by saying it, beckoning us towards a definition of Shakespearean comedy as a whole:

'Tis still a dream, or else such stuff as madmen
Tongue, and brain not; either both or nothing,
Or senseless speaking, or a speaking such
As sense cannot untie.

Further Reading

There is no standard critical commentary on Shakespeare's comedies. E. M. W. Tillyard, *Shakespeare's Early Comedies* (London, 1965) was left unfinished at his death, and therefore deals only with the early comedies. The three most widely available books on the subject are – H. B. Charlton, *Shakespearian Comedy* (London, 1938); John Russell Brown, *Shakespeare and his Comedies* (London, 1957); and Bertrand Evans, *Shakespeare's Comedies* (Oxford, 1960). None of these has a specialist audience in mind and none has a distractingly polemical purpose. So, in spite of their long-windedness and sometimes dullness, they do have something to recommend them to those who enjoy the comedies. Brown's is the best, in my opinion, though his opening chapter on 'Implicit Judgment', with its tedious generalisations about Shakespeare's methods of moral commentary, is best avoided. For a more vivacious and more scrupulous account of the comedies we have to look forward to the time when one or other of the very fine critics I list below assembles his essays on the subject in the form of a book.

Meanwhile there are several interesting books with a more specialist or polemical purpose. C. L. Barber, *Shakespeare's Festive Comedy* (Princeton, 1959) is a provocative account of aspects of festivity and 'game' in the comedies. I have referred to it in my Preface. M. C. Bradbrook, *The Growth and Structure of Elizabethan Comedy* (London, 1955) is useful for its description of the comic conventions Shakespeare adapted from customary Elizabethan practice. Northrop Frye, *A Natural Perspective* (New York and London, 1965) tries to revive our appreciation of the mythic and ritual basis of Shakespeare's comic art. E. C. Pettet, *Shakespeare and the Romance Tradition* (London, 1949) shows how Shakespeare adapted stories of romantic love to his own dramatic and comic requirements, and how, in doing so, he provided a critical perspective in which the audience is encouraged to view the fortunes of the lovers in the mature comedies. Two pamphlets in the Longman's series prepared for the British Council are worth reading – G. K. Hunter, *Shakespeare: The Later Comedies* (London, 1962); and Frank Kermode, *Shakespeare: The Final Plays* (London, 1963). For those who enjoy literary detective work, J. Leslie Hotson, *Shakespeare's Motley* (London, 1952) on the fool, and *The First Night of Twelfth Night* (London, 1954) make fascinating reading. There are volumes in the Macmillan 'Casebook' series on *The Merchant of Venice* ed. John Wilders (London, 1969), *Henry IV, Parts 1 and 2* ed. G. K. Hunter (London, 1970), *Twelfth Night* ed. D. J. Palmer (London, 1972), *Measure for Measure* ed. C. K. Stead (London, 1971), *The Winter's Tale* ed. Kenneth Muir (London, 1968) and *The Tempest* ed. D. J. Palmer (London, 1968). David R. Young, *Something of Great Constancy* (London, 1966) is a thorough critical interpretation of a single play, *A Midsummer Night's Dream*.

Other books on more general subjects contain interesting material on the comedies. Harley Granville-Barker, *Prefaces to Shakespeare* includes essays on *Love's Labour's Lost* (First Series: London, 1927) and *The Merchant of Venice* (Second Series: London, 1930). William Empson, *Some Versions of Pastoral* (London, 1935) discusses comic aspects of *Henry IV, Part 1*, *Troilus and Cressida* and *Measure for Measure* in two chapters, 'Double Plots' and 'They That Have Power'. Mark van Doren, *Shakespeare* (New York, 1941) is especially good on the comedies (it contains the best essay I have read on *As You Like It*). A. P. Rossiter, *Angel with Horns* (London, 1961) has some thoughtful comments on *Much Ado*, *All's Well*, *Troilus and Cressida* and *Measure for Measure*. John Russell Brown, *Shakespeare's Plays in Performance* (London, 1966) has useful information about the staging of *Twelfth Night*. D. J. Enright, *Shakespeare and the Students* (London, 1970) takes an irreverent look at *The Winter's Tale*. M. M. Mahood takes up what some might consider to be a more sensible, as well as a more reverent attitude towards the same play in her excellent *Shakespeare's Wordplay* (London, 1957).

Much of the best work on Shakespeare's comedies is to be found in essays and introductions to editions of the texts. *The Tempest* does very well from this point of view, with a stimulating as well as scholarly essay introducing Frank Kermode's Arden edition (London, 1954), and a brilliant critical-descriptive piece by Ann Righter for Penguin (Harmondsworth, 1968). Ann Righter's essay on *Love's Labour's Lost* (*Shakespeare Quarterly* IV, 1953) is also well worth reading, as is her more recent essay on 'Shakespeare's Sense of an Ending' in *As You Like It* and *Twelfth Night*. This last appears in 'Stratford-upon-Avon Studies' 14, *Shakespearian Comedy* ed. M. Bradbury and D. J. Palmer (London, 1972), which is full of good things on this subject. See especially J. Russell Brown, 'The Presentation of Comedy: the First Ten Plays' (better than his book on the comedies in my view); J. Dixon Hunt, 'Grace, Art and the Neglect of Time in *Love's Labour's Lost*'; and D. J. Palmer, '*The Merchant of Venice*, or The Importance of Being Earnest'. Two other particularly good 'Introductions' are Barbara Everett's to the Penguin edition of *All's Well* (London, 1970), and M. M. Mahood's to the Penguin edition of *Twelfth Night* (London, 1968). Barbara Everett has written interestingly on *Much Ado* in *The Critical Quarterly*, Winter, 1961, as has D. J. Palmer on '*As You Like It* and the Idea of Play' in *The Critical Quarterly*, Autumn, 1971. Another good essay on *Much Ado*, also appearing in *The Critical Quarterly*, Spring, 1967, is by John Wain, 'The Shakespearean Lie Detector: Thoughts on *Much Ado about Nothing*'. Frank Kermode has an essay on 'The Mature Comedies' in 'Stratford-upon-Avon Studies' 3, *Early Shakespeare* ed. J. R. Brown and B. Harris (London, 1961). Francis Berry has one on 'Word and Picture in the Final Plays' (very good on *Pericles*, and worth reading for what it says about *The Tempest*, too) in 'Stratford-upon-Avon Studies' 8, *Later Shakespeare* ed. J. R. Brown and B. Harris (London, 1966). For those especially interested in Shakespeare's stage there is an informative essay (by Daniel Seltzer in the same volume) called 'The Staging of the Last Plays'.

A last word about introductions to Shakespeare's work as a whole that will help to 'place' the comedies. I have already mentioned F. E. Halliday, *A Shakespeare Companion*, (Harmondsworth, 1964) in the Preface. I also recommend P. Quennell, *Shakespeare: The Poet and his Background* (London, 1963), a readable critical biography; John Wain, *The Living World of Shakespeare* (London, 1964), a good general guide to the plays; A. M. Nagler, *Shakespeare's Stage* (Yale, 1958), the best short account of its subject; and finally Eric Bentley, *The Life of the Drama* (London, 1965), for all those who wish to consider more carefully the nature and function of comedy in its relation to other theatrical genres.

I should add that many of the texts can be purchased in paperback editions. All the editions of separate Shakespeare plays I have mentioned can be obtained in paperback. Many of the books on Shakespeare are published in the Penguin Shakespeare Library.

Index